D1559270

PROPERTY OF A GENTLEMAN

The formation, organisation and dispersal
of the private library 1620-1920

PROPERTY OF A GENTLEMAN

The formation, organisation and dispersal of
the private library 1620-1920

Edited by

Robin Myers and Michael Harris

ST PAUL'S BIBLIOGRAPHIES

WINCHESTER

1991

© 1991 The Contributors

First published 1991 by
St Paul's Bibliographies
West End House
1 Step Terrace
Winchester
Hampshire SO22 5BW

British Library Cataloguing in Publication Data

Property of a gentleman : the formation, organisation
and dispersal of the private library 1620-1920.
I. Myers, Robin II. Harris, Michael, *1938-*
027.141

ISBN 0-906795-99-0

Cover illustration: "George Allen Esq^f, F.A.S.. William Hutchinson Esq^f,
F.A.S.". Frontispiece to John Nichols, *Literary Anecdotes of the Eighteenth
Century* (1812-15), Vol. *VIII*.

Typeset in CG Times by Ella Whitehead, Munslow, Shropshire
Printed in England by Henry Ling, Dorchester
Bound in England by Green Street Bindery, Oxford

Contents

Introduction

THE PAPERS of the twelfth annual conference on book trade history, held under the auspices of the Centre for Extra-Mural Studies, Birkbeck College, return to the theme of bibliophily, which we dealt with in our seventh conference (published 1986). The history of the private library will be hard to write. With the books almost invariably dispersed or absorbed into the maw of huge institutional collections, they only occasionally achieve coherent visibility. The immensely painstaking reconstructions involving the use of book-plates, shelf marks and a variety of other cryptic and idiosyncratic markings, have helped to identify a proportion of the libraries of such notable individuals as Richard Hooker, John Dee and Horace Walpole. Occasionally, hand-written lists made by the collector him- or herself can reveal in brilliant detail the form and content of a personal library. However, more often the only access to a private collection is through an auction catalogue, appearing like a meteor at the moment of dissolution. As a by-product of a commercial process, rather than a careful record of a life-time of painstaking accumulation, sale catalogues are full of *lacunae*. Blocked out with such tantalising phrases as 'a collection of pamphlets' or 'a quantity of old books' or containing anonymous properties mixed in with the books of a known collector, they remain gripping but enigmatic. The whole auction process is replete with ambiguities. 'Property of a Gentleman', the title of the conference and this book, is itself an evasive phrase sheltering a long succession of odd and disreputable individuals. This collection of original essays by leading specialists in the field of bibliography, some with extensive auction-house experience, draws aside the curtain to reveal some of the realities of individual collecting.

Who were these 'gentlemen' whose status was in some way closely linked to the quality and bulk of their libraries? Through a series of detailed investigations a variety of collectors emerge. David Stoker reveals in his study of 'Honest' Tom Martin, the 18th-century Norfolk antiquary, the fatal combination of acquisitiveness and drink. The picture of Martin, to whom books and manuscripts were a dominant and ruinous obsession, hiding his best volumes from an invited purchaser, is irresistible. Robin Myers describes an altogether more respectable collector in the person of William

Herbert, the distinguished bibliographer. She identifies the principles and techniques by which a City merchant turned country gentleman with considerable resources assembled and partially dismantled his collection. Rather different were the collecting methods of the manuscript collector, Henry Yates Thompson. In an enthralling study of his activities in the sale rooms during a very long life, Christopher de Hamel analyses the shifts in the reputation of this remarkable collector whose buying and selling at auction at the turn of the century involved a series of refinements of the phrase 'Property of a Gentleman'. Frank Herrmann, on the other hand, provides an insight into the career of Thomas Plume, one of the earliest English collectors to buy at auction. Starting with a description of how Plume assembled his library Frank Herrmann leads on to an account of the development of book-auctioneering and of the various pioneer auctioneers of the 17th and 18th centuries. On a broader front, contributors to this volume also investigate the phenomenon of the private library as an indicator of both taste and status. Using a number of 17th-century library catalogues, T.A. Birrell gives a marvellous view of the range and character of private collections before the formalisation of later periods set in. His investigation into what august 17th-century gentlemen considered light literature (what he describes as 'joco-serio'), indicates with considerable force the importance of this neglected category of material and reveals that the English gentleman was a good deal more polyglot than his present-day EEC descendant. Perhaps the most striking way in which collectors have attempted to define their status and perpetuate their association with an accumulation of books is through the use of book-plates. Brian North Lee gives a close analysis of the signs and symbols and heraldic devices deployed through these complex items and, with a lucid chronological account of gentlemen's book-plates, contributes to our knowledge of this too little-known area of book history, which he has made his own. Esther Potter approaches the subject from a different angle; she has accumulated a wealth of information on the changing fashion in bookbindings in libraries, and gives a fascinating account of the way in which gentlemen got their books bound and conserved in the 17th and 18th centuries.

During the conference a series of under-represented lines of research into the evolution of the private library emerged with some clarity – in particular, the issue of the changing layout and organisation of the private house. This was the main subject of the workshop session and Katherine Swift and Clive Wainwright provided valuable discussion papers on this theme. Unfortunately Katherine Swift has been prevented by ill-health from publishing her contribution, but Clive Wainwright's essay on the changing purpose of the library as a room often used as a kind of second drawing-room, analyses for the first time the evolution of the book-closet into the library with a special status in the gentleman's house.

Robin Myers and Michael Harris
London, 1991

Contributors

T.A. BIRRELL is a retired teacher of English and is presently engaged in compiling a catalogue of the Old Royal Library. His publications include *The Library of John Morris* and *English Monarchs and their Books*.

CHRISTOPHER DE HAMEL is a director of Sotheby's and in charge of the sale of medieval illuminated manuscripts. He is author of *Glossed Books of the Bible, The Origins of the Paris Booktrade* and of *A History of Illuminated Manuscripts*.

FRANK HERRMANN F.S.A. is founder-director of Bloomsbury Book Auctions. He worked for many years in publishing and is author of *The English as Collectors* and *Sotheby's: Portrait of an Auction House*.

BRIAN NORTH LEE is the author of numerous articles and six books on bookplates including *Early Printed Book Labels* and *British Bookplates*.

ROBIN MYERS is Hon. Archivist of the Stationers' Company in London. She is joint editor of the conference papers and has written extensively on areas of book-trade history. She published *The Stationers' Company Archive, 1554-1984, a Companion to the Records*, in 1990.

ESTHER POTTER is a former librarian who has recently catalogued the bibliographical papers of Graham Pollard. She is working on the Jaffray papers in the British Library, largely concerned with bookbinding.

DAVID STOKER lectures in the Department of Information and Library Studies at the University College of Wales. He has written extensively on the 18th-century country trade, and is currently editing the correspondence of the Norfolk historian Francis Blomefield.

CLIVE WAINWRIGHT is a Curator in the Furniture Department of the V & A Museum. He is the author of *The Romantic Interior: The British Collector at Home 1750-1850*.

List of those attending the Conference

Jean Archibald
Librarian

Iain Beavan

Ronald Browne
Librarian

Jackie Canning
Student

Paul Christianson
University teacher

Andrew Cook
Archivist

Karen Cook
Map librarian

Nest Davies

Sarah Dodgson

Michael Fielding

Keith Fletcher
Bookseller

Hans Fellner
Christie's

Myrjam Foot
British Library

David Hall
Librarian

Judith Harrison
British Library

Colston Hartley

John Hewish
Librarian

Katie Hooper
University of Liverpool

Ashley Huish
Librarian

Arnold Hunt
Research student

Mervyn Jannetta
Librarian

Graham Jefcoate
Librarian

Beverley Kemp
British Library

Jeremy Knight
Curator

Colin Lee

Anthony Lister
Retired teacher

Warren McDougall
Teacher

Giles Mandelbrote
Publisher

Stuart Morrison

The emergence of the book auctioneer
as a professional

FRANK HERRMANN

SOME 50 miles east of London lies the little East Anglian town of Maldon in Essex on the River Blackwater. It has a long history which is much studied. In fact, the town is about to celebrate a millennium, for in the year 991 a grim battle took place on the shores of the Blackwater in which, through a gentlemanly, but intensely stupid, gesture, the local chieftain lost the battle and was killed by invading Norsemen. We know this from one of the earliest extant poems in Old English.

Now the reason why Maldon is of interest to us today is that it was there in 1630 that Thomas Plume was born, the son of a local alderman. Young Plume went to the local grammar school in nearby Chelmsford and then to Christ College in Cambridge. He took his BA and MA in 1649, aged 19, became a Bachelor of Divinity in 1661, and a Doctor of Divinity in 1673. In 1658 he had become vicar of Greenwich, where he remained until his death in 1704, that is for 46 years. It is important to recall that he lived during one of the most turbulent periods of English history, with constant strife, civil war, and such major disasters as the Great Plague of 1665 and the Great Fire of London in 1666.

Plume appears to have been a convinced Royalist and committed Anglican but he never got into trouble.[1] In fact, he was appointed to the living in Greenwich by none other than Richard Cromwell. He subsequently became a confident and enthusiastic buyer of books, an activity which he seems to have carried on without a break for nearly half a century. The library he built up in this way was very much a working tool.[2] Like his early employer Dr John Hacket, Plume was a good preacher.[3] The delivery of sermons was among the most important tasks of the 17th-century Anglican clergyman. Pepys and Evelyn both made mention of Plume's excellence as a preacher after recording their attendance at his church in Greenwich in their diaries. 'A minister of religion', wrote James Thomas Oxley in 1609, preaching to his fellow clergy in Durham, should be 'the eyes of the world for his congregation to disperse the clouds of ignorance and give life.'[4] In

1

Plume's day, the fire and brimstone approach was no longer appropriate. We might remember that the bibliographical luminary, Thomas Frognall Dibdin, had commented that the divines in the late 16th and early 17th century who published commentaries 'had frequently worked themselves up into a whirlwind of indignation in what they conceived to be the conscientious discharge of their duties. The very leaves of their pamphlets seemed to smell of fire!'.[5] Even what C.V. Wedgwood called 'the staccato chime of Bishop Andrews and the tolling bell of John Donne'[6] were no longer in fashion. The politics of the time saw to that.

Plume bought and read books that covered every shade of religious, political, historical, and indeed scientific and philosophical, opinion.[7] He had an amazingly enquiring mind into most aspects of the growing corpus of knowledge. He had, for example, Harvey's first work on the circulation of the blood of 1649. Among a host of books on travel and geography he owned Thomas Mun's *Discourse of Trade in the East Indies*, 1621, and Thomas Neale's excessively rare *Treatise of direction on how to travel profitably into Foreign Countries* of 1643. He had Sir William Petty's *Essay Concerning the Multiplication of Mankind*, 1686, and Petty's earlier celebrated *Treatise on Taxes and Contributions*, 1662. Among some 1600 tracts and pamphlets,[8] Plume owned the infamous and thoroughly venomous *Decree of the Starre Chamber concerning Printing* of 1637 that ushered in what F.A. Mumby – because of its extremely repressive nature – calls 'the darkest age in the history of the English book trade since Caxton set up his press at Westminster'. Plume also possessed Milton's *Doctrine and Discipline of Divorce*, and the volumes by authors that came out in response to Milton's challenging attitude, *and* he had Milton's reply to those.

He had John Prynne's notorious, and notoriously dull, *Historio Mastix, or the Players Scourge* of 1633 and 35 of Prynne's 200 published pamphlets and books. He owned at one time the great poetry and drama of the period – works by John Donne, Francis Beaumont, Charles Cotton, Abraham Cowley, Sir Thomas Denham, Thomas Flatman, William Greenwood, George Harper, Thomas Heywood, John Milton, Francis Quarles, James Shirley, John Skelton, Edmund Spenser, Sir John Suckling and Edmund Waller. Books of biblical commentary, theological introspection and religious history dominated the publishing scene and predominated in most libraries in Plume's day, as they did in his own.[9] They were immensely popular with the general public and were often printed in editions which even present-day publishers would regard as very satisfactory. Most popular of all were sermons – some 8,800 saw the light of day in print between 1660 and 1750.

By the time Plume was approaching 70 he began to consider what to do with his earthly possessions. He never married and had no direct heirs. His library now numbered some 7-8,000 volumes and, after much reflection, he decided to leave it as a reference library to the place of his birth, the town of Maldon. But not only that, he determined to construct a building in which to house the library and to leave funds in perpetuity for its upkeep, replenishment and even for the employment of a librarian. You can see it in Maldon to the present day. It was, at the time, one of the first libraries to be made available to the general public.

One of the things that has puzzled us about Plume is where and how he acquired his books. We know that many of them are second-hand copies because we have earlier names on the fly leaves and the title pages. We know that in 1628 the Warden of the Stationers' Company compiled a list of 38 booksellers who also dealt with 'old libraries', i.e. second-hand books and 'mart books', that is importations from the Continent, usually selected and ordered from the great Continental book fairs at Frankfurt and Leipzig, Leyden and Cracow.[10] Presumably, by the time Plume was buying extensively, this source of second-hand books had increased. Plume may have been personally familiar with many of the leading theological authors of his time. Like him, they tended to frequent booksellers' shops and booths, which often served as something of a social meeting place. Plume was a great talent spotter, if only because he had often acquired the early books of the best of such authors when they were still relatively unknown, and *lacked* their major works which they published *after* Plume's death.

Conversely, we also have in the Plume Library a good many works by Dr Lazarus Seaman, the Rev. William Greenhill, Dr Thomas Manton, Gisbert Voet, Sir Kenelm Digby, Stephen Charnock, Dr Henry Stubb, the Rev. John Dunton, the Rev. Dr William Howell, the Rev. William Outram, John Warner, William Hawkins and David Stokes. What precisely – you might wonder – do these gentlemen, mostly clergy, represent? Intriguingly, it was *their* libraries which were sold by auction in the years 1676 to 1685, the first ten years of which we have book auction records in England. So there is at least a strong chance that Plume was one of the earliest purchasers at English book auctions.[11] The idea was imported from Holland where auctions generally, and book auctions in particular, had already been in use for nearly a century. (Presumably auctioneers were regarded as highly respectable in Holland, for did not Rembrandt paint a portrait of one – Thomas Jacob Haaring – now hanging in the Metropolitan Museum in New York?)

Many of the earliest English auction sales took place in the houses in which the libraries were situated. Later, the books were moved to coffee houses which had large rooms available for such functions. Later still, of course, but quite a bit later, auctioneers began to have their own premises. And who were the men who staged this new way of disposing of old books? By and large they seem to have been booksellers who realised that this was a relatively speedy method of disposing of stock. Though right from the outset it required what was probably considered an additional chore: namely, the compilation and printing of catalogues. The information given was of the simplest. Every title became a separate lot. All that was listed usually was the author's surname and an abbreviated title. Very soon the date of publication was also included: it was an easy way of pinpointing an edition. It was only many years later that the size of each volume was also given.

It is important to remember that, though there was a large inflow of books from the Continent, particularly at a time when Latin was a language universally understood – which made the publication of truly international editions a much simpler matter than it is today – the number of new publications which appeared in Britain each year was relatively small.

The first name on our list of authors known to Plume whose libraries were sold by auction, was that of Dr Lazarus Seaman. The auction was held on 31 October 1676 and was staged by William Cooper, a bookseller, in Dr Seaman's own house in Warwick Lane, conveniently close to the centre of the book trade. Cooper launched his catalogue with a *Note to the Reader*. Clearly a good deal of thought had gone into its compilation. As the principles outlined remained virtually standard for many years it is worth quoting in full:

READER
It hath not been usual here in England to make Sales of BOOKS by way of Auction, or who will give most for them: But it having been practised in other Countreys to the Advantage both of Buyers and Sellers; It was therefore conceived (for the Encouragement of Learning) to publish the Sale of these Books this manner of way; and it is hoped that this will not be unacceptable to Schollers; and therefore we thought it convenient to give an Advertisement concerning the manner of proceeding therein.

First, That having this Catalogue of the Books, and their Editions under their several Heads and Numbers, it will be more easie for any Person of Quality, Gentlemen, or others, to Depute any one to Buy such Books for them as they shall desire, if their occasions will not permit them to be present at the Auction themselves.

Secondly, That those which bid most are the Buyers; and if any manifest Differences should arise, that then the same Book or Books shall be forthwith exposed again to Sale, and the highest bidder to have the same.

Thirdly, That all the Books according to the Catalogue are (for so much as we know) perfect, and sold as such; But if any of them appear to be otherwise before they be taken away, the Buyer shall have his choice of taking or leaving the same.

Fourthly, That the Mony for the Books bought, be paid at the Delivery of them, within one Month's time after the Auction is ended.

Fifthly, That the Auction will begin the 31st of October at the Deceased Dr's House in Warwick Court in Warwick lane punctually at Nine of the Clock in the Morning, and Two in the Afternoon, and this to continue daily until all the Books be Sold. Wherefore it is desired, that the Gentlemen, or those Deputed by them, may be there precisely at the Hours appointed, lest they should miss the opportunity of Buying those Books, which either themselves or their Friends desire.[12]

There are three facts of particular note here: first, that commission bidding was permitted right from the outset; secondly, that the auctioneer allowed the return of imperfect books (presumably this was an extension of a practice common in second-hand book shops); and thirdly, that the auctioneer did not expect to be paid for a month after the sale. This implied that he retained the books until that time, which must have involved considerable clerical labour and storage capacity. The one thing we do not know – or shall I say, I don't know for certain – is whether the early auctioneers had actually bought the libraries they were selling. My belief is that in general they *had not*. Certainly Samuel Baker had not.[13] The issue is confused by a slightly different type of book catalogue which appeared very commonly in the early 18th century where the books were described as 'being sold cheap' and prices were given after each lot. These seemed occasionally to have been used as auction catalogues as well, and probably were of libraries or collections of books that were the auctioneer's property. A variant of these so-called 'retail' catalogues was also issued with the statement on the title page, 'Prices fixed and written in the books'. They are discussed at some length by Leonore Coral in her *British Book Sale Catalogues, 1676-1800*, and the first one that she came across is dated 7 February 1732.

Book auction sales were advertised in newspapers but I am only aware of such publicity in the 18th century when the growth of newspaper publishing was much further advanced. In the early days of auctions therefore catalogues were distributed by the auctioneer among other friendly booksellers so that the prospective buyer could pick them up.

The number of auctions recorded in the early days is very limited: there was one in 1676; two in 1677; six in 1678; four in 1679; seven in 1680; ten in 1681; only four in 1682; back to eight in 1683, and ten in 1684. By 1687 we reach 27, and numbers fluctuate at around that level or below it thereafter. They reached 30 in 1776 exactly 100 years after the Seaman sale. William Cooper, who had staged the Seaman sale, had held 23 book sales by 1688, that is, in 12 years, so clearly he found it a useful and profitable way of making an income additional to book selling, but obviously the work involved was such that two sales a year were enough for him. Between 1683 and 1686, he held occasional sales jointly with Edward Millington, who in due course became the most prominent auctioneer of his time and held some 98 book sales between 1680 and 1703. It is interesting that he branched out into the provinces. He held a sale at the Stourbridge Fair near Cambridge in 1684 and another in 1685, and others in Trumpington, Oxford, Cambridge, Norwich and High Wycombe. He also held a good many art sales and was credited with introducing a new system of artificial lighting which made the winter evening sales particularly attractive. He held a certain number of sales in Tunbridge Wells during the summer season 'for the diversion and entertainment of Gentlemen, Ladies, etc.', who had gone there to escape from the hurly burly of late 17th-century London; or perhaps the smells in London in high summer were too much for them. He must have died in 1703, for his own library is the first recorded sale in January 1704. It must also have been large because the second and third parts were not sold until the following year.

The next major figure to emerge among auctioneers was Thomas Ballard, between 1706 and 1734. He worked almost exclusively from a single site during this period, at St Paul's Coffee House. It was ideally situated at the very heart of the book trade at 'the corner of the entrance from Paul's Churchyard to Doctors Common'. Much later, the same coffee house became the venue of a dining club which met there on Thursdays, of which James Boswell was a prestigious member. Ballard held 86 auctions in all. His catalogues were quite often titled in Latin, and foreign and Latin books were an important part of what he sold. He is best remembered for the sale of the huge library of Thomas Rawlinson, FRS, sold in the record-breaking figure of 16 sessions over 13 years. Dibdin described Rawlinson as 'A very leviathan of book collectors'. His was the largest library up till then sold at auction and was said to include 200,000 volumes. The 16th part of the sale was confined to manuscripts, some 1,020 of them. Surprisingly, one of the principal purchasers at all these sales was Thomas Rawlinson's younger brother Richard, an even more omnivorous collector of books, who left the Bodleian some 5,700 manuscripts (and a great many particularly rare books as well) on his death. Richard's library was, in turn, sold in 1756 by an up-and-coming young auctioneer called Samuel Baker, but more of him anon. Richard Rawlinson, you may recall, was a barrister who lived in Gray's Inn and has his place in the history books because his four rooms in Gray's Inn were so stuffed with books that he was forced to sleep in the corridor outside.

A contemporary of Ballard's who was also very active as an auctioneer was Christopher Cock. Cock held some 38 book sales but achieved considerable fame in his day as one of the earliest and most successful art auctioneers. He had his own rooms at the Piazza in Covent Garden and in the sale of the picture collection of Sir Robert Cotton in April 1733, knocked down the nine huge tapestry cartoons by Andrea Mantegna, which had once belonged to the celebrated collection of Charles I – and are now to be seen at Hampton Court. Cock's most famous sale was of the art collection of the Earls of Oxford in 1741. Both father and son had also been prodigiously active collectors of books and manuscripts. On the death of Edward Harley, the Second Earl of Oxford, the entire library was bought by the bookseller Thomas Osborne (who generally used Cock when he wanted to sell something by auction). Osborne felt that the Harleian library called for a special catalogue and, indeed, for special cataloguing, with more explicit descriptions of each book than usual. The man he employed for this immense task – for there were in excess of 40,000 books – was the son of a country bookseller, one Samuel Johnson. The detailed scrutiny of so much diverse literature was to stand Dr Johnson, with his marvellously retentive memory, in good stead all his life. The first volume of the library catalogue contains a lengthy preface, in which Osborne apologises for putting such a catalogue on sale and actually charging for it, but he hopes that posterity will learn 'of the excellence and value of this great collection' in this manner. De Ricci (in his classic *English Collectors of Books and Manuscripts 1530-1930)* did not like it because the descriptions were too woolly and insufficiently bibliographical for his liking, although he appreciated that the Harley Librarian, William Oldys, had collaborated very fully with Johnson in his compilation. But more important from our point of view was that what many regarded as Johnson's model cataloguing was certainly closely studied by his contemporaries.

Another figure who is important when it comes to standards of cataloguing – although we are jumping ahead a bit – is Samuel Paterson (1728-1802). Paterson was famed in his day for his immense knowledge of the *contents* of books.[14]. He issued 'digested' catalogues, a practice he is said to have learned from the Paris bookseller, Gabriel Martin. Paterson was also one of the first cataloguers to identify varying editions and issues of the same title, particularly by English writers, in proper chronological sequence. He acted as an auctioneer for many years, sometimes in his own right, sometimes with a partner called Eve, between 1757 and 1787, but after going bankrupt took to cataloguing for other auctioneers and booksellers. For many years he also acted as librarian for the First Marquis of Lansdowne, who included within his library a particularly fine collection of State papers that had been largely got together by two earlier collectors, James West and Phillip Carteret Webb. (Although catalogued many years later by Sotheby's, it never came up at auction and was bought in its entirety by the British Museum.)

Paterson is probably best remembered for the fine catalogue of the wide-ranging and scholarly library of John Strange, which was used as a bibliographical model by others for many years because of its almost complete range of 18th-century publications.

At this point it is necessary to introduce a key figure in the auction trade, who, with his successors, stands as an epitome of the profession. His name was Samuel Baker. He became an apprentice to Richard Mallard, bookseller of St John's Lane, for an annual wage of £5 at the age of 15. In 1711 at the age of 22 he started issuing his own printed catalogues – not of auctions, but of priced stock. The first such catalogue appeared on 19 February 1733; two more appeared in April and November of the same year, and we know of ten altogether by the time Baker issued his first auction catalogue. This was of the valuable library of the Rt. Hon. Sir John Stanley, *Bt.*, and it was described as 'containing several hundred scarce and valuable books in all branches of Polite literature'. The sale was to be held over ten nights in the Great Room, over Exeter Exchange in the Strand, beginning on 11 March 1744. The conditions of sale are signed by Samuel Baker, Auctioneer, and by John Atkinson, Writer: writer in this context seems to indicate that he was the cataloguer because he signed a number of book catalogues issued by other auctioneers at about this period.

There were 457 lots, so each evening's sale must have been quite short. Baker's early book sales were organised by size: the octavos came first; then the quartos; finally the folios. Within each size the order of items was completely random; later it was to become alphabetical, as it was in Baker's fixed price catalogues. These also contain whole sections of duodecimos – known in the trade as 'twelves' because that was the number of pages that came out of a printed sheet when it was folded in a certain way. They were very popular for collected, multi-volume sets of established authors and thus ideal for libraries.

Important and potentially expensive titles were set in italics. Thus lot 186 of the library of Dr Richard Rawlinson, sold, as we already know on 29 March 1756, is printed as *A Treatyse Dyalogue of Dives and Paupers, that is to saye, the Ryche and the Poore. Emprinted by me Wynkyn de Worde at Westmonstre, 1486.* Major sales continued remorselessly for days – or rather evenings – on end: 40, even 50, continuous sessions were not uncommon and probably eliminated all but trade buyers. Even for them it must have required the patience of Job to sit right through them, night after night, for hard, wooden benches were all that was provided for buyers at such sales, as we can see from contemporary drawings. And it may be of interest to note that the Rawlinson sale included 9,405 lots, which fetched a total of £1,161 18*s*. 6*d*., that is an average of 2*s* 6*d*, or 12½p, a lot! This sale was spread over 50 sessions, so Baker's take at the end of each evening was £23 5*s*., of which he would only keep, say, 10% for himself as commission – and this was at a truly outstanding sale, so book auctioneering in general was not something that would lead to instant riches!

A second Rawlinson sale underlines this even more strongly. It was described as 'upward of 20,000 pamphlets, reduced into lots under proper heads'; it took nine days and raised £203.13*s*. 6*d*. Here the cataloguing was of the sketchiest. Lot 82 reads '17 tracts on various useful subjects'; lot 143 '21 voyages and travels, *chiefly old*'. There was a further Rawlinson sale of 'Prints, Books of Prints, and Drawings'. It lasted eight evenings and the catalogue mentions upward of 10,000 prints! 103 by Dürer fetched a mere £1 10*s*. 6*d*., and 24 etchings by Rembrandt, sold as four lots, realised £3. 5*s*. The total for the sale came to £163 10*s*. 3*d*. Baker seems to have realised that it was too much for the market to absorb at one time and he did not make the same mistake again.

Early on in his career Baker rarely held more than four sales a year and clearly his bookselling business still constituted the major part of his income. He also sold stationery, as one learns from advertisements in his catalogues, and, in the old tradition, he also occasionally acted as publisher. At the end of the Rawlinson catalogue he advertises 'An Essay towards a new English Translation of Job, from the original Hebrew, with a commentary; price 5*s*. sewed, by Thomas Heath of Exeter'. He was to auction Heath's library four years later. Here was true synergy! Baker also published a number of school text books. One of his most popular was 'A Treatise of Arithmetick in Whole Numbers and Equations wherein all of the necessary practical rules are laid down in the plainest and most familiar terms and the truth of each rule demonstrated'. He gives his imprint as 'Printed and sold by Samuel Baker, bookseller at the Angel and Crown, in Russel-street, Covent Garden'.

His terms and conditions of sale for auctions should be mentioned. They were the simplest in the business, and made other auctioneers' terms seem positively legalistic. (I have just had a Christie's catalogue which contains 34 *pages* of such preamble!) The conditions were usually printed on the back of the title page or on the page following, and read:

I.   That he who bids most is the Buyer; but if any Dispute arises, the Book or Books be put up to Sale again.

II.   That no Person advances less than Six-pence each Bidding; and after the Book arises to One Pound, not less than One Shilling.

III.   The Books are supposed to be perfect; but if any appear otherwise before taken away, the Buyer is at his Choice to take or leave them.

IV.   That each Person give in his Name, and pay Five Shillings in the Pound (if demanded) for what he buys; and that no Book be deliver'd in Time of Selling, unless first paid for.

V.   The Books must be taken away at the Buyer's Expence, and the Money paid at the Place of Sale, within three Days after the Sale is ended. [Clearly this is a major departure from Cooper's Conditions of Sale. Cash flow problems had reared their ugly head in the intervening 60 years!]

Any Gentleman who cannot attend the Sale, may have their [*sic*] Commissions receiv'd, and faithfully executed.

By their most Humble Servant,
SAMUEL BAKER

As Baker's business prospered – and contemporary accounts tell us that he was a very shrewd business man – he moved into premises of his own in York Street, Covent Garden, and there he remained for many years. By the 1750s St Paul's was no longer the essential book trade magnet it had once been.

The first sale from the new premises, and probably the most memorable, was of the library of Dr Richard Mead, the most brilliant physician of his time and an indefatigable collector of books, curiosities and works of art. Major libraries continued to come Baker's way, the fame of the business spread and by the time he reached 50 years he held as many as one-fifth of all the book auctions that took place in London each year. By the time he was 55 he clearly felt he had to enlarge his small staff with a young partner who could carry on the business after him. The young man he chose was the 25-year-old ninth son of a Canon of Hereford Cathedral, named George Leigh. Leigh must have had a good knowledge of the book world because the style of the firm changed to BAKER AND LEIGH very soon after Leigh arrived. A subtle change in the style of cataloguing also becomes discernible almost at once. For the first time we see lots which include more than one title, a habit other book auctioneers had adopted some time earlier. There are occasional detailed bibliographical comments on particularly noteworthy aspects of the books included.

Sam took it easier, built himself a 'delightful villa' at Woodford Bridge near Chigwell in Essex, but sadly lost his very supportive helpmate and wife, Rebecca Flitcroft, soon after. In April 1769 came the accolade of being asked to dispose of duplicates from the British Museum. In 1778 he spent two weeks at Woburn Abbey, cataloguing the Duke of Bedford's library, and later that year he died.[15] Leigh had become a full partner in 1774, and in his will Baker appoints two bookseller friends to share the stock-in-trade of the firm between Leigh and Baker's nephew, John Sotheby. Sotheby was 38 when he joined the firm and it seems that he looked after administration while George Leigh became the auctioneer. The style of the firm changed to LEIGH AND SOTHEBY and ultimately, three generations of the Sotheby family were at its helm until 1861.[16]

Baker's choice of Leigh as helpmeet, successor and tutor to John Sotheby was brilliantly contrived. Leigh was universally liked. He was a good auctioneer and it seems evident that he gave the business the additional sophistication and expertise it needed at a time when, under a particularly enlightened monarch, George III, the interest in collecting, literature and the arts received unusual encouragement. Leigh and Sotheby's catalogues became noticeably more elegant in the 1780s and 1790s. The detail of the cataloguing improved also, and the prices, particularly of manuscript material and prints, rose gently; but none of this would have been possible without the solid foundations laid by Samuel Baker. His energy and integrity stood out prominently in the cut and thrust of London's vigorous book trade of that period, and he survived and thrived where so many others had gone to the wall. It seemed particularly apt, therefore, that Samuel Sotheby (John's son) should refer to Baker, the leading book auctioneer of his time, as the 'Father of our Tribe' when he discussed him with Dibdin years later.

George Leigh himself died in 1816, still in harness after nearly 50 years in the business. He seems to have been an amusing, lively, fair-minded man who gave the relatively dull commerce of book auctioneering an extra dimension of pleasurable anticipation and continuous excitement. The era from 1770 to 1816 was important in the history of book collecting. It saw an increasing interest in early English and Elizabethan literature and a waning in the obsession with the Greek and Roman classics, as well as with the Italian books which had been so highly regarded in the middle of the previous century. A greater interest in manuscripts of all kinds – particularly as historical source material – became discernible and the detail of books began to be more closely studied with corresponding advances in bibliographical description. Book prices too began to rise, but up to the third quarter of the 18th century it is difficult to make out any rationale in the value of antiquarian books.

Up to that time most books published during the century sold for ten shillings or less, and the more esoteric books from earlier eras sold at between ten shillings and £1, but in matters concerning the book trade at this stage there were exceptions to every rule and very little true conformity. It was a rare lot indeed that rose above two guineas and as a rule that would be a heavily illustrated work of reference in many volumes. After 1780 a price of £20 was not that exceptional. Leigh and John Sotheby were well aware of these trends and their catalogues mirrored them conscientiously, though the number of auctions held was still very limited.

As far as a pattern of trading becomes perceptible, Leigh and Sotheby liked to hold the bulk of their sales in the first half of the year, with the occasional sale in December. Presumably the second part of the year was devoted to selling the contents of their fixed-price bookseller's catalogue (it included nearly 10,000 items by 1799) and to the firm's publishing activities which seem to have grown extensively by the end of the century. There were no fewer than seven pages of titles advertised in the same 1799 catalogue.

Before we finish with Leigh I should tell you that, like my own dear partner, Lord John Kerr, Leigh took snuff. It played an important role in his life and to quote the antiquarian Richard Gough, who wrote in 1812, 'His pleasant disposition, his skill and his integrity are as well known as his famous snuff box. When a high priced book is balanced between £15 and £20, it is a fearful sign of its reaching an additional sum, if Mr Leigh should lay down his hammer and delve into his crumpled horn-shaped snuff box'. A little later the Pall Mall bookseller, William Gardner, wrote a long eulogy of Leigh (after Dibdin had described him in something of a teasing piece), 'During a space of forty years devoted to the service of the public [Leigh] has attended to its interests, whatever might be the magnitude, with the utmost vigilance, impartiality and success; and in a profession accompanied by much trouble, perplexity, confusion and uncertainty, has spared neither his person nor purse to introduce regularity, method and precision; and has preserved a character not only unstained and unsuspected, but highly honourable. His discharge of duty during the hour of sale cannot be too

highly praised .....'
Truly, a great professional had emerged.

References

1. W.J. Petchey, *The Intentions of Thomas Plume*, (an expanded version of the 1981 Plume Lecture, and an invaluable source book of information on Dr Plume), Maldon, 1985.
2. Frank Herrmann, *The Importance of Books to Dr Plume*, the Plume Lecture, 1990, (to be published).
3. John Hacket, Bishop of Lichfield and Coventry, *A Century of Sermons*, published by T. Plume, London, 1693. STC (Wing) H.169. Hacket left his sermons to Plume, who published them in a magnificent folio volume with a lengthy, if slightly sycophantic, introduction.
4. Quoted in Victor Gray, (Essex County Archivist), *Honey and Wormwood: Voices from the Pulpit in Dr Plume's Day*, the Plume Lecture, 1982, (unpublished).
5. The Rev. T.F. Dibdin, *The Library Companion*, second edition, London 1825, p.53.
6. C.V. Wedgwood, *17th Century English Literature*, London 1950: a neglected classic that gives a wonderfully pithy and concise conspectus of the life and literature of the period described.
7. There are five major inventories of the Plume Library stock. The first was the briefest of lists which accompanied the books, all packed in barrels, when they were shipped from Greenwich to Maldon after Plume's death, and they were checked by the Master of the Maldon Grammar School, one M. Scarrow, on 29 November 1704. The second was compiled by Robert Hay, who doubled up as Master of the Grammar School and Plume Librarian, in 1761. The third was the work of the Rev. Robert Crane, vicar of Heybridge, in 1843. He was at various times a Trustee of the Library as well as Librarian, and titled his inventory 'Duplicate Catalogue of the Books in Archdeacon Plume's Library'. The Rev. Andrew Clarke, vicar of Great Leighs, and one of the most diligent and industrious in the long line of Plume Librarians, produced a catalogue of the 1600 pamphlets in the Library in 1903. (See also note 8.) Finally, S.G. Deed, Headmaster of the Grammar School in Maldon, and Plume Librarian for many years, produced the definitive printed catalogue in 1959 with the assistance of Jane Francis. This is still in print (price £10).
8. As well as compiling the catalogue of the pamphlets, the Rev. Andrew Clarke described them in some detail in an article in *The Essex Review*, Vol XII, 1903, pp.159-165.
9. See the invaluable article on 'Biblical Criticism, Literature, and the 18th Century Reader' by Thomas R. Preston in *Books and their Readers in Eighteenth Century England*, edited by Isobel Rivers, Leicester University Press, 1982.
10. See Cyprian Blagden, *The Stationers' Company: a History, 1403-1959*, London, 1960, p.121, n.1.
11. Frank Herrmann, Plume Lecture 1990.
12. Quoted here from Anthony Hobson's foreword to *British Book Sale Catalogues, 1676-1800*, a Union list compiled and edited by A.N.L. Munby and Leonore Coral, London, 1977.
13. Interesting evidence to this effect came to light in the paper by David Stoker 'The ill-gotten Library of "Honest" Tom Martin' (printed below, pp.103-4) in a letter from Ducarel to Thomas Martin dated 4 May 1762, in which Ducarel suggests Samuel Baker to be 'the

properest person' to sell Martin's library by auction, and that Baker may 'advance money upon the collection', but makes clear that this is a loan against a sale by auction and *not* a part of any purchase price.

14. Much of the information on Paterson and book auctions of this period generally, but Samuel Baker and George Leigh in particular, is drawn from the early chapters of the author's *Sotheby's: Portrait of an Auction House*, London and New York, 1980, which covers the history of the book trade and book collecting in the 18th century in detail.

15. Baker held 99 sales in 34 years.

16. For the different styles used by the firm, see *A List of the Original Catalogues of the Principal Libraries, which have been sold by Auction*, which Samuel Leigh Sotheby compiled in 1828. It was later used as a sales catalogue for 'A Series of 146 Volumes in Quarto, with Prices and Purchasers' Names', part of the firm's own archive, disposed of during a period of particularly acute economic hardship in 1831.

The library as living room

CLIVE WAINWRIGHT

THE PLANNING of houses both in town and country was evolving and increasing in complexity throughout the 18th century. Architects and their clients were constantly changing their ideas concerning the role of each room within a house. For instance, as the hour and the nature of dining changed so did the desiderata for a modern fashionable dining room and its furnishings. The functioning of private libraries as rooms has been to some extent discussed in print[1] though curiously the country house library is absent from the recent exhaustive examination of most other aspects of country house life.[2] In this essay I shall briefly examine a few aspects of this complex subject.

Naturally the form of the domestic library was also affected by changes in the expectations and habits of its users. Libraries have always been more than just repositories of books; for instance, collections of curiosities, sculpture and works of art have naturally gravitated towards them. Quite apart from the celebrated books and manuscripts, by the 1620s the Cotton Library included curiosities such as coins, medals, precious stones and a fossilised fish.[3] William Stukeley wrote in 1751 'I have adorned my study with heads, bas-reliefs, bustos... I look upon myself as dead to London, & what passes in the learned world. My study is my elysium'.[4]

Even for moderately bookish persons and particularly for scholars and antiquaries, the library had since the 16th century been a room in which they spent a great deal of time – by any definition a *de facto* living room. Thus as the authors of the Classical world filled the shelves in profusion so the presence of Classical antiquities, as in Stukeley's case, or representations of the heroes of the Classical world were wholly appropriate as furnishings. In some cases such representations performed a functional role also, as in the well-known case of the Cotton Library where the press-marks were dictated by the placing of Classical busts; '... by the late 1630s the library was housed in fourteen presses, five or six shelves to a press, each surmounted by a brass head of one of the twelve Caesars from Julius to Domitian, of Cleopatra or of Faustina'.[5]

It might be argued that these busts were just part of the decoration of the Library like the long tradition of portraits of worthies painted on library walls and ceilings. Such painted decoration is, however, a separate tradition with a long Continental history, and even in this country it starts at least as early as the portraits of authors, such as Chaucer, painted in the frieze of the Bodleian in about 1616.[6] The same tradition runs well into the 19th century with, for instance, the heads of worthies painted by Crace in the 1840s above the bookcases in the Lower Library at Chatsworth.[7]

As soon as free-standing three-dimensional sculpture begins to adorn a library, whether on the bookcases or elsewhere in the room, and is allied to curiosities as in the Cotton Library, the room begins to function as more than just a place for books alone. Naturally visitors gravitated towards it and lingered in it to socialise with one another. By the mid-18th century comfortable library chairs and sofas along with several writing tables began to be supplied as standard furnishings. This encouraged visitors to congregate in the library and chairs were indeed provided for this very reason. A lone bibliophile needs no more than a chair and a table in his library – however large – and probably little cares whether the chair is comfortable. Such bibliophiles of course used their libraries as their main living room, as Montaigne charmingly described in the 16th century as far as his own country house was concerned:

...I thence see under me my garden, court and base court, and almost all parts of the building...'Tis in the third story of a tower, of which the ground floor is my chapel, the second story a chamber with a withdrawing-room and a closet...the figure of my study is round and there is no more open wall than what is taken up with my table and chair, so that the remaining parts of the circle present me a view of all my books at once ranged upon five rows of shelves round about me. It has three noble and free prospects, and is sixteen paces in diameter.[8]

A little thought concerning the practicalities of country house life helps to explain this enhancement of the role of libraries. Whilst the weekend house party only really became widespread with the arrival of the railway, considerable numbers of guests had always come to stay at country houses. Indeed even before the railway it was quite practical to travel down for the weekend to houses in the home counties or in the environs of, say, Edinburgh or Bristol. The guests might be a miscellaneous bunch with widely differing interests or they might be carefully chosen by the host or his wife so that they could plot a cabinet reshuffle, the appropriate marriage of a child or the launch of a new canal company. However, they expected to be entertained. Eating and drinking, of course, played an important role in which all took part, but how to fill the rest of the time? The best thing was to get them out of the house altogether; this, often, was achieved by organising hunting of almost anything that ran, flew or swam. But even here our weather frequently presented problems and there were always those too unfit, unwilling or lazy to take part.

Where could the guests congregate indoors, especially in bad weather? The drawing room was a possibility for tea or perhaps a little light reading in the afternoon, but not appropriate for morning use; consequently the library came more and more to serve purposes not fulfilled by the dining or the drawing rooms. An interesting sidelight on such use of a famous Regency library is provided by the descriptions of the 'Topographical Gatherings' which Sir Richard Colt Hoare held at Stourhead in Wiltshire from just before 1820 until 1833. Colt Hoare:

Always hospitable, always liberal, always generous and kind he had long been accustomed to receive at his house persons of literary tastes and habits; but now the hospitality assumed something of a more systematic character...these assemblies were accustomed to expect a summons for the September week, from Monday to Saturday...to the more studious of the party, and especially to those who had not easy access to so rich a collection of printed books, the library afforded sufficient employment; to the lover of the fine arts, the collection of pictures, for which the house at Stourhead is so renowned; while the gardens abounded in attractions for the botanist; and the beauty of the walks through the grounds....[9]

John Skinner the antiquary, archaeologist and vicar of Camerton in Somerset described one of these convivial events which took place in early January 1824. After being delayed by snowdrifts he arrived at Stourhead to find that:

...dinner was over; but the worthy owner of the mansion left the company to see proper care taken of me, and after a hearty meal on a smoking hot beef steak I joined the party...after coffee we had a rubber of whist, in which I came off a gainer of 7s...I was downstairs a little after eight, and in the library in order to make references. Mr. Offley soon after joined me, and Mr. Charles Bowles of Shaftesbury who is engaged in one of the Wiltshire hundreds... After breakfast we assumed our stations in the library, and I soon perceived my associates, although their pursuits were in a different beat were not less eager than myself after antiquarian game, and we occupied the first part of the morning without any kind of interuption till we were summoned to take refreshments in the dining room....[10]

These gatherings were largely organised for the antiquaries and topographers who Colt Hoare knew through his own research into the history of Wiltshire, all of whom would wish to make considerable use of the library during their stay. The library however needed to be appropriately designed and furnished to accommodate far more people than the owner and his immediate family. It fortunately still exists, with the splendid Grecian style mahogany furniture manufactured for it by Chippendale the younger still *in situ*.

That other celebrated bibliophile, Earl Spencer, not content with just one library like Colt Hoare, created a whole series of them at Althorp not only to house his rapidly growing collection of books, but (if we are to believe Dibdin) to serve also as living rooms. Dibdin even illustrates the 'Interior of the Long Library' with guests entertaining themselves:

The figures introduced will also give a notion of the usual purposes to which this room is devoted; namely as a Morning Sitting Room, or Drawing Room; and is indeed considered the usual place for assembling, either morning or evening, by the visitors...In the evening as before observed, it is used as a *Drawing Room*; where the company assemble on rising from the dinner table...THE BILLIARD LIBRARY This room is so called, from the billiard table being placed in the middle...THE MARLBOROUGH LIBRARY...is commonly used as an Evening Drawing Room for the family when they are alone...THE GOTHIC LIBRARY...Sofas, chairs, tables of every commodious form, are of course liberally scattered throughout the room.[11]

There is ample evidence, in novels as well as in diaries and letters, of families using the library as a living room. In 1849 Mrs Gore in one of her novels describes how it was in the library that the family '...spent their mornings, the hum of well-bred chat seemed to do its part in producing a genial atmosphere: half a dozen work tables and writing tables being in play in various nooks of the room, with praiseworthy activity of small-talk and Berlin wool'.[12] This must have been a library of reasonable size to accommodate six tables in use at one time.

Writing in the early 1820s the American author Washington Irving describes an event in the library at his imaginary old English mansion, Bracebridge Hall:

We arranged ourselves to hear the story. The captain seated himself on the sofa, besides the fair Julia...Lady Lillycraft buried herself in a deep, well-cushioned elbow chair. Her dogs were nestled on soft mats at her feet; and the gallant general took up his station, in an arm-chair at her side, and toyed with her elegantly ornamented work-bag. The rest of the circle being all equally well accommodated, the captain began his story.[13]

Interestingly, Irving visited Walter Scott at Abbotsford a few years earlier in 1816 and described an evening spent with Scott before his grand new library had been built.

After dinner we adjourned to the drawing room, which served also for study and library...The evening passed away delightfully in the quaint-looking apartment, half study, half drawing room. Scott read several passages from the old romance of Arthur, with a deep sonorous voice the gravity of the tone seemed to suit the antiquated black-letter volume.[14]

When Scott created a proper library at Abbotsford in 1824-1825 he also intended it to be used for more than just housing books. He wrote: 'But a house such as I was able to build in respect of extent had not space enough to afford a drawing room exclusively for social functions. The library is...a well-proportioned room, but unless varied by some angles it would want relief, or, in the phrase of womankind, would be inexcusably devoid of a flirting corner. To remedy this defect an octagon was thrown out upon the northern side of the room'.[15] Scott in conjunction with Atkinson his architect cleverly arranged matters so that the drawing room and library were next to each other so that when the drawing room was '...inadequate to the accommodation of our fair friends, especially if dancing or a musical party be in contemplation, we have only to open the door between the drawing room and library in order to obtain all the space necessary for the purpose...'.[16]

Scott could afford to allow his library to be used in this way whilst if he wished he could write in a calm quiet atmosphere, for opening off the library but separated from it by a stout door was '...the *Sanctum Sanctorum* of the all creating author of *Waverley*. The room was plainly furnished, with a table and a couple of chairs, and bookshelves all round, full of books *in use*, not in ornamental bindings like those in the large library'.[17] This formula of a library for show and social use and a study for scholarly work became as we shall see a frequent Victorian device when planning houses.

In another celebrated collector's house, Charlecote Park in Warwickshire, in the 1830s, a wing was added by the owner George Lucy to the original Elizabethan house, prompting a visitor to remark that 'The new apartments consist of a dining-room and drawing room serving also as a library'.[18] There is considerable evidence that it was thought particularly appropriate for the great halls and libraries in both ancient houses and those in the ancient British styles such as Gothic, Tudor or Elizabethan to be used by families and their guests as it was imagined that they were in 'days of yore'. Indeed that bible of the early Victorian creators of new and the improvers of genuinely old houses, Joseph Nash's *The Mansions of England in the Olden Time*, depicts both libraries and halls being used in this way.

In 1864 the definitive book on the planning of houses was published and its title tells all: *The Gentleman's House; or how to plan English Residences, from the Parsonage to the Palace with tables of accommodation and cost, and a series of selected plans.* The author was Robert Kerr the architect, architectural writer and professor of the Arts of Construction at King's College London. In 1865, just after the publication of his book, Kerr designed and built Bear Wood in Berkshire for John Walter, the proprietor of *The Times*, and embodied in it his elaborate and sophisticated concepts of house planning. The book had a great influence upon both architects and their patrons and many later Victorian houses closely followed the principles put forward by Kerr.

Kerr's suggestions for the design and use of libraries are of considerable interest and must therefore be quoted at some length. In his chapter on the library he states that:

The degree of importance to be assigned to the Library in any particular house would appear, theoretically, to depend altogether upon the literary tastes of the family, and to be, indeed so far, a criterion of those tastes...It is not a Library in the sole sense of a depository for books. There is of course the family collection; and bookcases in which this is accommodated form the chief furniture of the apartment. But it would be an error, except in very special circumstances, to design a library for mere study. It is primarily a sort of Morning-room for gentlemen rather than anything else. Their correspondence is done here, their reading, and in some measure, their lounging; – and the Billiard-room, for instance is not infrequently attached to it. At the same time the ladies are not exactly excluded...The Fireplace ought to be placed so as to make a good winter fireside, because this is in great measure a sitting-room... Intercommunication is frequently made with the Drawing-room, and sometimes intimately and this carries with it no doubt a certain sort of convenience, because the two rooms can be thrown together occasionally for the evening.[19]

In a special chapter called 'Great Library; Museum Etc' Kerr describes how for the architect

It sometimes becomes necessary in a first-class Mansion to provide accommodation in a stately manner for a very extensive collection of books...involving perhaps the introduction of sculptures and paintings of a suitable kind...As regards curiosities and other artistic and scientific collections these may very properly be accommodated, whether in upright cases to correspond with the bookcases, or in cabinets to take the place of the reading tables.[20]

Such a library furnished with works of art, curiosities and – as so often is the case in country houses – with archaeological items excavated on the estate, would naturally attract most of the guests to the house.

The spate of books for amateurs, decorators and architects published in the second half of the 19th century frequently provide fascinating information on the use of rooms, including libraries. Kerr was used as source by many of the later authors including Henry Hudson Holly the New York architect who lifted whole sentences from Kerr – naturally without acknowledgement – for his book *Modern Dwellings* of 1878. In the chapter on the library as adapted for American use Holly makes some interesting if hardly original observations:

Probably the library more than any other room in the house, reflects the master mind of the household. One person regards this apartment as simply a place in which to read newspapers, write letters, and keep slippers and a dressing gown. Another's idea is that it is a museum for bric-a-brac, with showy bookcases and ample shelving for books purchased by the yard. The real library is, of course that in which the style and selection of reading matter convey some idea of certain specialities to which the dilettante or scientific possessor is prone...Home libraries, acting as a sort of rendezvous for social intercourse, may be far more cosy and inviting if arranged like a lady's boudoir.[21]

Thus from its beginnings in this country as the small private book-lined room of the 17th century scholar the library had become by the later 19th century a reception room almost interchangeable with the drawing room or morning room. Those few house owners of a really scholarly or literary disposition were able to create a *Sanctum Sanctorum* away from the attentions of their house guests. One only has to browse along the shelves of the average country house library – few metropolitan examples on any scale survive – to see that those who congregated in most libraries were sadly not much given to serious reading. Indeed, 'In more leisurely days when visitors came for a month and when winter mud made the surrounding lanes all but impassable, self-sufficiency in reading matter assumed an importance which it is difficult to envisage, and those long runs of *The Gentleman's Magazine*, *The Quarterly Review* and *Punch* (often relegated to the billiard room) were not mere interior decoration'.[22]

This growing use of the library as living room also had implications for the furniture created for it. The scholar's library required a solid pragmatic desk or table and a practical ladder or, even better, oak lectern style library steps with a reading surface so that one could relax and read whilst at the top. But as soon as tribes of house guests or indeed one's own large family were wont to congregate there a whole range of furniture was needed – comfortable armchairs for sleeping away a winter afternoon between lunch and tea; elegant leather-covered writing tables for writing casual letters; sofas on which to sit whilst reading the illustrated periodicals and serialised novels laid out so invitingly on the sofa-table itself; a folio stand or two next to the sofa containing fashionable popular prints; perhaps a round centre table with an oil lamp standing in the middle so that several people could sit around it and embroider, read and chat the evening away. I have even heard of card-tables being provided in particularly un-bookish libraries.

The fashionable library was often furnished with overtly 'clever' furniture such as library steps that fold out of flimsy neo-Classical satinwood tables, ladders which fold into poles, or the patent mahogany 'Metamorphic' library chair which converts into steps – all of which provide far too unstable a perch for the serious scholar wishing to consult a massive ancient quarto on an upper shelf. The treads of such steps are usually covered in the same carpet as the library floor and there is usually a notable lack of wear when one examines them even after 150 years of possible use.

The best surviving illustration I have found of a library wholeheartedly designed and furnished as a living room for the entertainment of a large number of guests is reproduced opposite. This shows the splendid Gothic Revival Library at Eaton Hall in Cheshire in 1882 as created for the Duke of Westminster by Alfred Waterhouse, the architect of the house. There is a splendid range of comfortable chairs both modern and antique as well as tea tables and writing tables in sufficient quantity to satisfy 30 or 40 guests. There is even a grand organ in case background music was needed during tea or perhaps an evening recital. There are actually a considerable number of books on the shelves, but they do not dominate the room to say the least and there seem to be no library steps. Singular though the provision of an organ in a library theoretically devoted to quiet pursuits may seem this practice had a certain vogue in ducal households at this period; the end of the library at Blenheim is still dominated by the immense organ built by the celebrated Father Henry Willis in 1891 for the Duke of Marlborough.

In the final analysis, though it may be perhaps still fashionable to entertain in one's own library, which as I have shown has been the case

The library at Eaton Hall, 1882

since the late 18th century, I suspect that many of my readers would be more at home in a cosy and private *Sanctum Sanctorum* like that described by Scott:

One end was entirely occupied with bookshelves, greatly too limited in space for the number of volumes, placed upon them...while numberless others littered the floor and the tables, amid a chaos of maps, engravings, scraps of parchment, bundles of papers, pieces of old armour... Behind Mr Oldbuck's seat (which was an ancient leather covered easy-chair, worn smooth with constant use) was a huge oaken cabinet...a large old-fashioned oaken table was covered with a profusion of papers, documents, books...In the midst of this wreck of ancient books and utensils, with a gravity equal to Marius among the ruins of Carthage sat a large black cat....[23]

References

1. Mark Girouard, *Life in the English Country House* (London, 1978). Peter Thornton, *Authentic Decor* (London, 1984).
2. *The Fashioning and Functioning of the British Country House* ed. Gervase Jackson-Stops, et.al. (Hanover & London, 1989).

3. Kevin Sharpe, *Sir Robert Cotton* (London, 1979), p.66
4. Bodleian Library MSS Eng. Misc. c.538.f.7.
5. Thomas Smith, *Catalogus librorum manuscriptorum bibliothecae Cottonianae* ed. C.G.C. Tite (Cambridge, 1984), p.5.
6. André Masson, *The Pictorial Catalogue Mural Decoration in Libraries* (Oxford, 1981), p.5.
7. Megan Aldrich, *The Craces. Royal Decorators 1768-1899* (London, 1990), Plate 9.
8. *The Essays of Michel de Montaigne* ed. W.C. Hazlitt (London, 1892), III, p.46.
9. 'The Topographical gatherings at Stourhead, 1825-1833'. *Archaeological Institute Proceedings, Salisbury* (1849), pp.22-26.
10. *Journal of a Somerset Rector 1803-1834*, ed. H. & P. Coombs (Bath, 1971), pp.257-258.
11. Thomas Frognall Dibdin, *Aedes Althorpianea or An Account of the Mansion, Books, and Pictures at Althorp* (London, 1822), I, pp.20-31. The Plate illustrating the interior of the Long Library faces page 20.
12. Catherine Gore, *The Diamond and the Pearl* (London, 1849), I, 288. Quoted by Jill Franklin in *The Gentleman's Country House and its plan 1835-1914* (London, 1981), p.46. This book has an excellent section on libraries.
13. Washington Irving, *Bracebridge Hall* (London, 1845), p.121.
14. Washington Irving, *Abbotsford and Newstead Abbey* (London, 1835), pp.42-45.
15. Monica Maxwell Scott 'Sir Walter Scott on his "Gabions"', *The Nineteenth Century* (1905), LVIII, pp.782-783.
16. *ibid.*, p.785.
17. *Life and Letters of William Bewick Artist* ed. Thomas Landseer (London, 1871), II, p.251. I have illustrated and discussed the study, library and drawing room at Abbotsford at length in *The Romantic Interior: The British Collector at Home 1750-1850* (London, 1989).
18. Samuel Carter Hall, *The Baronial Halls and Picturesque Edifices of England* (London, 1848), II, p.4.
19. Robert Kerr, *The Gentleman's House* (London, 1871), third ed., pp.116-117.
20. *ibid.*, pp.188-189.
21. Henry Hudson Holly, *Modern Dwellings in Town and Country Adapted to American Wants and Climate* (New York, 1878), pp.107-108.
22. A.N.L. Munby, 'The Library', in *The Destruction of the English Country House 1875-1975*, ed. Roy Strong et.al., (London 1974), pp.106-107.
23. Walter Scott, *The Antiquary* (Edinburgh, 1816), I, pp.51-53.

'To Paul's Churchyard to treat with a bookbinder'

ESTHER POTTER

THE CONSENSUS of opinion was that the Douce books were lovely to look at. Mrs Humphrey Ward, when she was 17 years old, had seen the Douce collection in the Bodleian library in Oxford, and she retained for ever a memory of the golden light of the room. She recalled in her memoirs that it seemed 'to be the mingled product of all the delicate browns and yellows and golds in the bindings of the books'.[1] Whether she knew it or not, she was echoing Dibdin who had seen those same books on Francis Douce's own shelves and admired their 'soft and warm glow'.[2]

Now this golden glow is not achieved without some trouble taken by the owner and his bookbinder, or a previous owner and binder; for a collector would not need to have all his books newly bound. The owner of a country house library inherits books from previous generations, and even a collector starting *de novo* would buy many books ready bound. Edward Gibbon's library was rich in recently published English and French belles-lettres, history, science and current affairs, but he said that his books were chiefly collected from public sales, and, like many collectors, he wanted them 'to be dispersed in the same way so that they will be again culled by various buyers according to the measure of their wants and means'.[3] Stationers were selling second-hand books before Caxton, and, from the late 17th century onwards, a succession of sales of famous libraries offered opportunities to the connoisseur.

The buyer of a *new* book had several options when it came to the binding. Until the 19th century when publishers assumed responsibility for binding the whole edition of a book, most books reached the bookseller from the printer in sheets. Some copies would be kept in that form for those who preferred their own binding, and some the bookseller would have bound to display on his counter and to sell to those who wanted a book ready bound. And the customer would have a choice of bindings. One day Samuel Pepys went to Martin's, his bookseller, to buy the new edition of *L'escole des Filles* – and was dismayed to find that it was decidedly pornographic. He had little difficulty in convincing himself that it was his duty to read it, as

25

he said, 'to inform myself in the villany of the world'. But unlike Sir Edward Bysshe who had a copy, Pepys would have been ashamed for it to be found in his catalogue or standing on his shelves; so he bought it 'in plain binding (avoiding the buying of it better bound) because I resolve, as soon as I have read it, to burn it'.[4]

We cannot check what this plain binding was like because Pepys finished reading the book next day and he *did* burn it before supper. But there is documentary evidence for the range of bindings available from the booksellers in those price lists which Dr Mirjam Foot described at this conference in 1984.[5] They are prices agreed by the bookbinders among themselves and later with the booksellers for trade binding, that is the usual styles produced at the time for booksellers to keep in stock. The 17th-century lists show the normal styles of calf bindings, plain or decorated in blind or gold with filets, corner and centre blocks or oval stamps. From these standard bindings a collector could furnish his shelves adequately for use, but not for show. There is no mention of velvet, which was much used for grand bindings in the early part of the century, nor of goatskin, which became popular later; for these, and for elaborate gold tooling, a special binding would have to be commissioned, either through a bookseller or direct from a binder. Decorative tooling on the spine was not common before the latter part of the 17th century, but then it became popular along with lettering on the spine, and these are provided for in the 18th century lists.

Later in the 18th century the book collector would be studying catalogues like the one Alexander Donaldson issued in 1764 with this note on the bindings: 'To accommodate everybody, they [the books] are bound in various forms, some in turky[6] with gilt leaves [i.e. edges], and bordered with gold on the edges; others in calf and lettered. Such as chuse them unbound, may have them in sheets, sewed or in boards.'[7] To the buyer there was no essential difference between a book in sheets, sewn or in boards; they all had their edges uncut in the expectation that they would eventually be given a permanent binding, and then the edges could be trimmed without unduly reducing the margins. The advantage to the bookseller of a book sewn or in boards was that it was easier to handle than sheets, and the purchaser could conveniently read it before deciding whether it was worth the expense of binding.

The bookseller's turkey, which Donaldson mentions, was not always to be despised. The names of some well-known binders appear in booksellers' advertisements. William Pickering's catalogue no.2, issued in the spring of 1825 or thereabouts, offers his Diamond Classics, 10 pocket-sized volumes, in boards for £2.17s the set, or bound in morocco by Hering for £4.7s. Benjamin White's catalogue of 1779 lists the four volumes of Thomas Pennant's *British Zoology*, 1776-7, in boards at £4.4s, 'bound new and neat' at £4.14s.6d, or 'elegantly bound by Baumgarten' at £5.5s. Dr A.N.L. Munby counted 67 works in that catalogue in Baumgarten bindings; some were second-hand books and may have been bound for a previous owner, but three-quarters of them were new publications.[8] Johnson, another prominent binder of the day, who numbered Michael Wodhull among his clients, did a great deal of binding for the bookseller Thomas Payne.

Towards the end of the 18th century a few of the larger booksellers were feeling their way towards binding up the whole edition of books they published and not just the copies they sold in their own shops. John Newbery was irritated that booksellers to whom he sold the fifth edition of Cordier's *Colloquia* in sheets, were selling copies in inferior bindings, which detracted from the reputation of the book; and so he determined to sell school books only in the strong linen binding he had devised.[9] No doubt it was similar reasoning which prompted Peter Boyle, an enterprising estate agent and publisher, to have bound in red roan his *Fashionable Court Guide*, a pocket directory of the nobility and gentry of London and Westminster which he started in 1792. It made sense to sell an annual directory ready bound since only an exceptionally fastidious user would put into morocco a book he was going to discard at the end of the year when the new edition came out. John Newbery bound children's story books in Dutch floral paper and Sir Richard Phillips issued his guide books in green roan. These early excursions into edition binding were limited to the kind of book that was expected to have a relatively short life. The tradition that works of literature should be soundly bound in leather persisted far into the 19th century.

The collector who bought a book in sheets or boards would have to decide how he wanted it to be bound. He would not lack advice. Gabriel Naudé, librarian to a succession of eminent collectors, published in 1627 *Avis pour dresser une bibliothèque*, which was conveniently translated into English by John Evelyn, the diarist, and himself a discriminating collector.[10] Naudé included some advice on binding and gave, somewhat unexpectedly, as his fourth rule, 'to cut off all the superfluous expenses which many prodigally and to no purpose bestow upon the binding and ornaments of their books … it becoming the ignorant onely to esteem a Book for its cover.'[11] Evelyn himself ignored this: his books are beautifully bound and elegantly gilded. So did Pepys (though Evelyn had given him a copy); and so apparently did everybody else who could afford it, for this was the golden age of English bookbinding and who could resist a copy of *The Gentleman's*

Calling, or something of that kind, bound in morocco and elaborately gilded all over in a delicate filigree pattern? One suspects that booksellers kept one or two displayed on their counters to tempt customers who, like Pepys, had a weakness for fine bindings. Pepys went to Westminster 'to Nott's the famous bookbinder that bound for my Lord Chancellor's library,[12] and here I did take occasion for curiosity to bespeak a book to be bound, only that I might have one of his bindings.'[13]

In fact Naudé's idea of a modest binding was not altogether austere – calf or morocco 'gilded with filets, and some little flowers, with the name of the Authors';[14] and what he was principally castigating was the habit, popular in France from the 16th century onwards, of having the pages of a book washed and ruled in red ink (or in gold on very special books). This seems to be a survival from the rubrication of manuscripts, and in the same way was the responsibility of the binder – if not to do it himself, at least to arrange for it to be done. Medieval college accounts frequently show separate amounts for the parchment and for writing the text, but illuminating and binding are often charged together in a single sum. Ruling was very popular in England in the 17th century. Pepys had books ruled in red. John Brindley, advertising his 1744 edition of the *Lives* of Cornelius Nepos, said: 'Such as desire, may have the Four Volumes ruled with Red Lines for 2s.6d extraordinary'.[15] As late as the 1770s Count MacCarthy employed Richard Weir and his wife to bind his books and Mrs Weir (who had quite a reputation for this art) ruled them.[16] Dibdin, like Naudé, deplored the habit.

New books would naturally be bound in the current style. But what of old books? Fashions in book collecting affected binding policy. Mr Anthony Hobson summed it up neatly when he observed that in the Henry E. Huntington Library incunabula which had come from Central European abbeys were in medieval bindings, while those from the aristocratic libraries of France and England were bound in 18th-century morocco.[17] In England in the 17th century collectors tended to have a scholarly objective, amassing books for their own researches, like Elias Ashmole and Anthony Wood, or to enrich public libraries, like Sir Thomas Bodley and William Laud. At the beginning of the 18th century the collecting of incunabula was the current fashion among wealthy noblemen: then for half a century the scholars held the field. Bibliomania returned in a more virulent form around 1780 and reached a peak at the Roxburghe sale of 1812. It is no surprise that this period coincided with another high spot in the history of English bookbinding. German binders flocked to London where there were wealthy collectors who could afford morocco and a lot of gold tooling, and who didn't quibble about the price.[18]

Some at least of the scholars had a taste for old books in their original binding. The Earl of Pembroke bought the Barocci collection of Greek manuscripts for the University of Oxford, of which he was Chancellor, and despatched them to Oxford via William Laud, at that time Bishop of London, with these instructions: 'Amonge these manuscripts theare are some that want bindinge. Mye lord would have them bound plaine and as like their old felowes as maye be.'[19] William Roscoe, supervising at the beginning of the 19th century the restoration of the Holkham manuscripts, many of which lacked covers, declared a similar policy: 'In case the ancient binding is in any tolerable condition it is better to preserve it than to change it for the finest modern binding.'[20] But in periods when book collecting was the fashionable craze of the nobility the library was an important part of the decor of a stately home and that required sumptuous bindings. The best account of the day-to-day management of a library in this tradition can be found in the entertaining diary of Humphrey Wanley, librarian to Robert Harley, first Earl of Oxford, and his son Edward.[21] The hall-mark of a gentleman's library was a collection of Greek manuscripts – and nothing was too good for them. As soon as the boxes had been unpacked and the books examined, they were despatched to the binder to be rebound in morocco.

There were a few exceptions to the policy of wholesale rebinding. The work of the great French binders was naturally cherished as it was, and Dibdin uttered one word of caution. He was talking about Elzevirs in limp vellum: 'When you find a book in this garb, think *twice* before you venture to exchange it for the venetian morocco of Charles Lewis.'[22] This was probably not because a vellum binding is a lovely thing in itself, nor because it is an excellent foil for its morocco neighbours on the shelf, but because Elzevirs were valued for the size of their margins, and despite all the pleas and threats of their clients, bookbinders *would* trim the leaves too heavily. 'Oh! the havoc I have seen committed by binders. You may assume your most impressive aspect – you may write down your instructions as if you were making your last will and testament – you may swear you will not pay if your books are ploughed – 'tis all in vain.' That was William Blades.[23] The other regular complaint was about the lettering on the spine, and one can have some sympathy with the binder. In an incunable the title is buried in an intricate colophon. 17th-century works of scholarship were apt to have a crowded title page in Latin with a great deal of extraneous information. So the prudent owner pencilled on a flyleaf the lettering he wanted – and still they got it wrong! Humphrey Wanley always provided a title for the spine and yet his diary is full of entries like this: 'Mr Elliot brought back most of the last parcel; but I returned four of the books to have the erroneous lettering amended.'[24]

It is a widely accepted convention that all the volumes of a multi-volume work should be bound alike, but it is not universal. The great French binders of the 16th century had no inhibitions about putting a different pattern on each volume of a set. There are six different designs on the covers of a ten-volume *Erasmus* of 1580 that was bound for Thomas Wotton,[25] and Mr Ehrman had the 1543 Estienne edition of Cicero's speeches in three volumes, also bound in Paris for Wotton, with different designs on each volume.[26] But English binders sometimes went to a great deal of trouble to match the later volumes to earlier ones where a work came out over a period. And this happened frequently. Take the case of Gibbon's *Decline and Fall*. It was a best-seller from the day of publication: no gentleman's library could be without it, but the owner would have to be quick off the mark to achieve a set in the same format, let alone uniformly bound. The first edition of volume I was published in February 1776 and sold out in a fortnight. The second edition followed in June and half of that was sold in three days. These were in quarto. If the collector could not wait for the next quarto editions of 1777 and 1778 he would have to make do with the Dublin piracy later in 1776, which was in two volumes octavo. Volumes II and III, published in quarto in 1787, would range with the London editions but not with the Dublin octavos which would have to wait for the Dublin piracy later in the year. At this stage no one, not even Gibbon himself, knew whether there would be any more. Volumes IV, V and VI appeared, in quarto, in 1788, twelve years after volume I, and Cadell and Davies had to reprint the first three volumes the following year to go with them. The first time that the whole work was printed at the same time was in 1791 when Cadell and Davies brought out an octavo edition in twelve volumes. No wonder there are so many sets of the *Decline and Fall* around with carefully matched but not quite uniform tooling.

Publication by subscription, which became popular in the 17th century, often created the need for this sort of matching, if the work were in several volumes. Subscription was much resorted to by authors who published their own works, and for books that were expensive to produce, such as works with many illustrations. The usual terms were payment of part of the price on subscription and the balance when the work was completed. Subscribers normally received their copies in sheets. Completion of the work not infrequently took longer than anticipated, and could lead to difficulties. Robin Myers told me of the correspondence on this topic between William Herbert, who was acting as his own publisher for his revised edition of Ames's *Typographical Antiquities*, and a subscriber, William White, who

lived in Wales and who seems to have traded on an acquaintance with
Herbert to get sheets as they came from the press. After waiting from 1780,
when the prospectus was issued, until 1784, White wrote to Herbert to
enquire after volume I and said he would 'wait patiently your own time for
the other two Vollums which God grant you may have time to finish. And
hope I may live to see.' In 1787 he was enquiring after volume III, having
meantime received volume II. In January 1790 he had part of it, and in 1793
he had volume III up to page 1740. In 1796 he reported that 'there wants to
compleat my set of books three plates. And I have more then belongs to me
6 sheets of letterpress containing Mr Ames preface from page 1701 to 1740.
These errors may have been occasion'd by my receiving the Book down in
peace meals as it was printed.'[27]

Of course they were! More experienced publishers were aware of the
danger. Subscribers to a multi-volume Bible received this notice.

'Though for their security and private use, they may have their copies in their own
possession till all be finished, yet they are to take notice that the Prefaces and some
other things which belong to the first Volume cannot be Printed till the whole work
be done, ... and therefore they are not to binde up their Copies, or disperse them,
but to keep them entire in their own Hands, that they may have all perfect at the last,
though for their private use, and to prevent the danger of loosing any Sheets if they
be loose, they may have them sowed ... together with Pastboard covers at a little
charge.'[28]

A development from publishing by subscription was publishing in
regular instalments. The issue of large and expensive works in parts, weekly
or monthly, began with Moxon's *Mechanick Exercises* in 1678 and was in
full swing in the 1730s. Many prestigious works appeared in this way
including a reprint of Palladio's *Architecture*, William Oldys's *Biographia
Britannica*, the *Harleian Miscellany*, the second edition of Johnson's
Dictionary, Chambers' *Cyclopaedia* and so on – so many in fact that the
Gentleman's Magazine printed a list of the serials currently in progress and
the stage each of them had reached.[29] Here again the buyer would need to
keep the parts carefully until the work was complete before having them
bound; though with subscription books and with part-issues he would
sometimes have the option of taking the complete work when printing was
finished in the publisher's binding.

The successful binding of a periodical requires a long-standing relationship with the binder. The *Gentleman's Magazine* began in 1731 and arrived
in blue wrappers once a month for more than 120 years.[30] I have seen a
complete run in only two bindings. The first 67 years are uniformly bound,

in 18th-century half green roan – not all at the same time because there are two changes of lettering tools; but leather, marbled paper for the boards and layout of the lettering on the spine have been carefully matched. Bibliographers, of course, are happy when this partnership breaks down, and the parts emerge from the back of a cupboard a couple of centuries later, still in their original wrappers.

Patrons of bookbinding were not content to have the whole of a multi-volume work bound uniformly. They went out of their way to put together sets of books with some common link and give them identical bindings. William Pickering advertised among his second-hand stock the four Shakespeare folios uniformly bound in russia. A very neat set could be achieved by dismembering collected volumes of short works and giving each individual piece a uniform binding, as did the Marquess of Bute with his famous collection of English plays. The trade was happy to encourage this propensity. John Brindley printed at the end of his 1744 edition of the *Lives* of Cornelius Nepos this advertisement:

'A sufficient QUANTITY of the above Classics for the CURIOUS, will be kept ready bound in Morocco, Blue Turkey, white *Cambridge* Bindings &c. marbled on the leaves ... And as there will be many volumes of the Classics, printed Patterns will be kept of the three different Sorts of Bindings that Gentlemen may have them all bound uniform, both as to Size, different Leather and Ornaments, without having Occasion for any of the Volumes being sent as a Pattern.'

This passion for uniformity often induced a patron to call in his bookbinder to work over a whole library. Graham Pollard in 'Changes in the style of bookbinding' described some of the forms this reworking took.[31] But there were other motives too. 16th-century and 17th-century books were not, as a rule, lettered on the spine but, as libraries grew, the need for identification arose, and wholesale labelling was done. John Evelyn was largely responsible for introducing into England the French style of binding with panelled sides and closely gilded spines incorporating a title. Pepys must have seen Evelyn's very elegant books when he visited him in November 1665. Pepys's own books at that time were in rather plain brown calf, piled up on chairs, and the one he wanted was always at the bottom of the heap. So he sent for the Navy joiner, Thomas Simpson, who devised for him the earliest known free-standing glazed bookcases; and then Pepys went 'to Pauls churchyard to treat with a bookbinder to come and gild the backs of all my books, to make them handsome, to stand in my new presses.'[32] That was on 13 August 1666, and it is fortunate that the bookbinder did not collect the books straightaway because three weeks later fire was sweeping through all the shops around St Pauls and Pepys had to find another binder.

Pepys wanted his books to look handsome. Another demand was for them to have some mark of ownership. In the days when books had silver clasps it was common for aristocratic owners to have their arms or a cypher engraved on the clasps. As books proliferated, a cheaper technique was required, and the custom arose of stamping the owner's arms or cypher on the sides, or the spine, or both. It served also as a simple but striking form of decoration. Of course the stamp had to be added to the old volumes as well, if there was a convenient space; and if the volume already bore someone else's arms a thin piece of leather in a contrasting colour would cover them up. The owner's name or initials served for those who had no arms. It is not to be supposed that famous binders spent all their time making fine bindings for posterity to admire. Charles Hering, round about 1810, had a stack of books to impress with Lord Petersham's arms, for which he charged him two shillings a volume if they were on both covers and in gold, and one shilling in blind.[33]

Then there were rows of periodicals that were *not* uniform and had to be put right. One member of the Kelly family had such a provoking time making uniform some volumes of the *General Acts and Statutes* that he kept the piece of paper with the instructions.[34] It reads:

> 35 Geo 3 }   now in quires, to be bound like volume 16 and
>   to   }   lettered volume 17
> 38 Geo 3 }
> The binding of 'Vol.1' 39 Geo 3 to 41 Geo 3 to be altered
> to correspond with vol.17 and lettered vol.18.
> 41 Geo 3 }   now in quires to be bound like pattern volume 2
>   to   }   and lettered vol.1
> 43 Geo 3 }
> The binding of vol.22 (11 G4 to 2 & 3 W4) to be altered to
> correspond with pattern volume 2 and to be lettered vol.12.

After that it was simpler: 'Bind up to correspond with pattern vol.2, volumes 13-20 – quires to come from the warehouse.'

This illustrates another service which bookbinders were called upon to provide – acquiring the sheets of a book which their patrons wanted them to bind. Tobias Smollett wrote to his publisher, James Rivington: 'Dear Sir, My neighbour John Lewis, bookbinder alias Strap, wants the Copies of the history which are bespoke by his customers – the money will be returned as soon as he can deliver the books. But he will expect to have them at

Booksellers prices. Will you let him have them accordingly and oblige Dr Sir, Yours sincerely, T^s Smollett.'[35] It appears that John Lewis did not normally act as a bookseller as well as binder, since he did not expect to receive as a matter of course the discount allowed to booksellers.

Pepys went to St Pauls Churchyard to look for a bookbinder. After the Fire many of them moved westwards and stayed there to be near their patrons who were building fine new houses in Holborn and Westminster. There was a saying in the trade: 'The West End binds for gentlemen and the City binds for the trade.' This reflects the fact that bookbinders tended to specialise either in binding single works for private clients or in bulk binding for publishers, and the trade binders naturally returned after the Fire to the City where the publishers had their warehouses. But the distinction was not clear-cut. As long as books were bound by hand there was no essential difference between fine binding and trade binding: the distinction lay in the care and time taken and the quality of the materials used. As we have seen, some of the fashionable West End binders did a good deal of work for the booksellers. The real break came with the development of machine blocking on case bindings from the 1830s onwards, when craft binding and machine binding needed different equipment and different skills. Even then it was a considerable time before specialisation was complete. Westleys and Company, one of the largest trade binders in the 19th century, had a department for 'Extra' work until 1873 when they transferred their private customers to Kelly and Sons who had decided to give up trade binding and concentrate on work for private clients.[36]

Those who lived in London, or who regularly visited London, would have no difficulty in finding a good binder at any period, but it would not have been easy to have especially elegant binding done before the 18th century outside London and a few other cities. There was a tradition of fine binding in Oxford and Cambridge from the middle ages onwards and Edinburgh could produce sumptuous velvet bindings for the Scottish kings in the 16th century. Elsewhere binders, with a few exceptions, were producing only simple serviceable bindings until about 1700. After that, excellent binders were widely spread. Charles Ramsden collected provincial bindings. He recorded the names of nearly 2,000 binders who were actively engaged in the trade in England and Wales outside London, and a further 700 in Scotland and Ireland.[37] It is clear from his own collection that many of them were more than just competent. 18th-century Edinburgh bindings are famous and so are those produced in Dublin in the 18th and early 19th centuries. After that Irish binding seems to have declined. A mid-19th century report recorded that many books were being sent to London for binding and that numbers employed in the trade had fallen dramatically.[38] Binding, like printing, came very late to Wales and most collectors had their binding done in London, Dublin, Shrewsbury or Chester.[39]

There was a great deal to be said for having books bound locally if it could be done. Transport was slow, hazardous and expensive. The London wagon that served William White's home in Wales left London on Saturday morning and did not reach Crickhowell until the following Friday. White was not alone in stressing the need for very careful packing to avoid damage on the journey. Printers hesitated to risk sending a whole impression in one consignment.[40] In 1652 postage on a letter was 2d up to 80 miles. Packets of printed books were charged two shillings a pound which might well double the cost of a book.[41] When Gibbon was living in Lausanne and ordering books from London he asked for them to be sent in sheets to minimise the cost of carriage.[42]

Setting up one's own bindery must have appeared an attractive solution to the transport question. It also helped with the question of supervision, which was a perennial problem. William Laud in his instructions to the University of Oxford about those Barocci manuscripts from the Earl of Pembroke said:

Mye Lord was once purposed to have them bound heare [in London], but it was hard to find whome to trust with them or whome wee should put to that paines to be a continuall overseer. If they should be mesplaced in the bindinge, it wear as much as manye of them wear worth, it would be soe hard to rectifye them againe. I thinke thearfore the safest waye will be to page them before they be taken asunder for newe bindinge.[43]

A private collector would have to operate on the scale of Peiresc to keep a first-class binder fully occupied, and some owners settled for installing their regular binder in their own house for limited periods. The Harleys had a workshop fitted up in their house in Dover Street, and insisted that Thomas Elliot bound their most precious manuscript, the *Codex Aureus*, there, at least until the leaves were secured in the right order in the new binding. He was then reluctantly allowed to take it away to do the tooling in his own workshop. Elliot did other jobs occasionally at Dover Street, and both he and Christopher Chapman, the Harleys' other regular binder at this time, were also persuaded to work for a few weeks at Wimpole Hall, the country house where most of the printed books were kept.[44] The Holkham Hall accounts show that on more than one occasion the binder John Robiquet was installed there for some months at a time, with his wife who presumably did the sewing and headbanding, his assistant and all his equipment; and, when the job was finished, everything was packed up again, presses and all, and they returned to London.[45] Count MacCarthy had a similar system; he took Richard Weir (who was at one time in partnership with Roger Payne) and Mrs Weir to his house in Toulouse to repair and bind his library.[46] Archbishop Parker installed printers as well as bookbinders at Lambeth Palace in the 1570s and binding was done there for perhaps three years.[47] The one private bindery that achieved a long life, and is still in operation after more than 200 years, was that of King George III. Previous royal collectors had patronised the best binders of the day, and the title 'Book-binder to the King' did not imply that the binder worked exclusively for the monarch. George III at first had his books bound by James Campbell in the Strand. Round about 1780 he decided to have his binding done 'in house', and he employed John Polwarth, Campbell's finisher, to supervise a bindery. The King took a good deal of interest in the bindery, which was situated in Buckingham House. When he came to visit the bindery the journeymen were usually aware of his coming in time to put on clean aprons kept for the purpose, but he occasionally caught them unawares cooking sprats over the fire, and was even more interested.

John Evelyn hints at amateur bookbinders. He left for his grandson, who was his heir, notes on how to manage the estate, and these have been edited by Sir Geoffrey Keynes. After talking about the library, Evelyn goes on: 'Also you should take Care of the *presses*, standishes, & Instruments belonging to writing, Desks, stamps, Seales, Skrew-presses, All the Tooles belonging to the Binding of Bookes, Cyfers, Coats of Armes, stamp letters, figures, Gilding tooles, Glew-pots, Cizers, Knives, &c all of which you have store.' He continues: 'This of bookbinding some gentlemen have been very expert in and excercised now and then themselves.'[48] If only he had told us who they were – and whether with all this equipment, he was one of them! He did read to the Royal Society one of the best accounts ever written of how to make marbled paper.[49] Another intriguing bequest is in the will of William Horman, Headmaster of Winchester 1495-1501 and then a Fellow of Eton until his death in 1535. He left his bookbinding tools to the College butler.[50] Eiluned Rees has recorded the names of some amateur Welsh binders who were no doubt driven by the dearth of professional binders to bind their own books.[51] The great period for amateur binding was the late 19th century. Apart from semi-professionals like T.J. Cobden-Sanderson and Sarah Prideaux, the best known is Sir Edward Sullivan who preserved in his photographs and rubbings all we now have of the magnificent bindings on the Irish Parliamentary volumes that were destroyed in 1922. In his own binding he avoided the time-consuming business of forwarding by having books bound for him, so that he could tool them, which is much more fun. He was an accomplished finisher.

Having got his books bound to his satisfaction, the owner then had the problem of looking after them. Those early collectors thought of everything. This is Bishop John Cosin of Durham, who had been in exile in Paris with John Evelyn during the Commonwealth: 'In winter the books should be all rubbed once a fortnight before the fire to prevent moulding.'[52] Naudé also had advice about furbishing: 'you may have recourse ... to the Binder, to repair the backs and peeled covers, restitch them, accommodate the transpositions, new paste the Mapps and Figures, cleanse the spoiled leaves, and briefly to keep all things in a condition fit for the ornament of the place and the conservation of the Books.'[53] Repairs of this sort were all in the day's work to the bookbinder and 19th-century binders regularly advertised 'libraries repaired and beautified'. But not all the bookbinder's work was done on printed books and manuscripts. Gibbon's bookbinding bills are mainly for new binding and the occasional repair, but included are batches of notebooks, a portfolio and four boxes made to look like books, two folio size, one quarto and one octavo. This seems to have been Gibbon's solution to the problem of pamphlets which Naudé and Evelyn preferred to have bound up in volumes.[54] Indeed any kind of box or case covered in leather, even telescopes, were liable to be decorated with gold tooling by a book binder. Round about the time of the Great Exhibition of 1851 pocket books and writing cases were in great demand, and some finishers were occupied in tooling gold borders on strips of leather to go on the edges of book-shelves.

It is difficult to generalise about the cost of binding. Before the use of machinery a trade binding in calf might add perhaps one-third to the cost of the book in sheets. Limp vellum would be cheaper. A bespoke binding in morocco could equal the cost of the text and a really elaborate one would be a good deal more. There is no upper limit to the cost of a fine binding. Cleaning and repairing the leaves of an old book was expensive, as Roger Payne's bills show. In the early days clasps were a costly item, and their maintenance even more expensive. Sir Thomas Bodley provided his library in Oxford with an elegantly bound benefactor's book. Twenty-five years later Mr Berry the goldsmith was repairing or regilding one or both of its clasps in six years out of seven at a cost of 2s.6d each clasp.[55]

Apart from the general trade price lists binders had their own lists for bespoke work. They do not seem to have costed each book separately, but calculated the price, for a similar style, according to the size of the book –

so much for a duodecimo, so much for an octavo and so on. This is natural since the most expensive item, until this century, was the cost of the leather, and the amount needed is determined much more by the size of the page than by the thickness of the book. Gibbon's binder in Lausanne routinely charged him, for binding new books in half roan, 8 sous for duodecimo and octavo, 16 sous for quarto and 32 for folios.[56] As we saw from John Brindley's advertisement, binders would keep a selection of bindings from which customers could choose a style.[57] Their standard charges would relate to those patterns and anything outside that range would be liable to an extra charge.

The recurring passion for uniformity might be supposed to produce shelf upon shelf of red morocco, or whatever; but with a few exceptions this is not so. Libraries which have accumulated over several generations and have passed through successive fashions for limp vellum, brown calf, morocco, sprinkled calf and russia would exhibit a pleasing diversity. It is possible to analyse the bindings of John Evelyn's library as it would have appeared in his lifetime. His books, most of them, remained in the family until they were sold at auction not so long ago, and they can be distinguished from those added by later members of the family because Evelyn almost always left some indication of his ownership. He and Sir Richard Browne, his father-in-law whose books he inherited, had similar tastes in binding, formed during a long stay in Paris during the Commonwealth. New books they had bound to their own taste, not all identical, but with a similar panel design on the boards, the spine closely gilded with the title, and their cypher or arms on the boards or spine. Evelyn preferred mottled calf; Sir Richard Browne more often chose morocco. Evelyn evidently agreed with Naudé to the extent of avoiding unnecessary rebinding. Almost all the books printed before about 1650 are in their original binding, nearly all in limp vellum with a few in calf (including one fine French binding). Special books, many Bibles, were in morocco. Evelyn received a good many presentation copies and those, of course, he did not have rebound. A sample count shows that this particular gentleman's library, about the year 1700, had two-thirds of its books bound in calf or sheep, mostly calf, with the rest fairly equally divided between morocco and vellum.[58]

The final result must have been not unlike the ideal library described by another great book lover, the Earl of Crawford and Balcarres: 'Uniformity robs us of what is perhaps the richest and most extended range of colour in the world – a wall space generously furnished with books, each clothed with its appropriate personality of varied style and hue, displaying the pride and ingenuity of different craftsmen, the reflections of successive fashion and taste but all combining with irresistible art to radiate light and shadow.'

References

1. *A writer's recollections*, 1918, p.112, quoted in Sir Edmund Craster, *History of the Bodleian Library 1845-1945*, Oxford, 1952, p.17.
2. T.F. Dibdin, *Bibliographical Decameron*, 1817, II, p.530.
3. *The letters of Edward Gibbon*, ed, J.E. Norton. 1956, III, no.803.
4. *Diary of Samuel Pepys*, ed. Robert Latham & William Matthews, 1970, entries for 8 and 9 February 1668.
5. Mirjam Foot, 'Some bookbinders' price lists of the seventeenth and eighteenth centuries' in *Economics of the British Booktrade 1605-1939*, ed. Robin Myers and Michael Harris, Cambridge, 1985, pp.124-175. I am also much indebted to Dr Foot for reading this paper and making constructive criticisms.
6. *Turkey* is a fine tanned goatskin imported from the Levant.
7. *A Catalogue of Books printed for Alexander Donaldson, bookseller in Edinburgh; and sold at his shop near Norfolk-street, in the Strand, London and at Edinburgh; and by the booksellers of Great Britain, Ireland and America*, Edinburgh: 1764.
8. A.N.L. Munby, book review in *The Book Collector*, 1, 1952, p.271.
9. Advertisement in *London Chronicle*, 14-17 January 1769, quoted in S. Roscoe, *John Newbery and his successors*, Appendix II.
10. John Evelyn, *Instructions concerning erecting of a library*, London, 1661. (new Wing N 247).
11. Ibid, p.61.
12. The Earl of Clarendon, author of the *History of the Rebellion*, to whom Evelyn had dedicated his translation of Naudé.
13. Pepys, *Diary*, 12 March 1669.
14. Evelyn, *Instructions*, p.84
15. *Cornelii Nepotis Excellentium imperatorum vitae*, Londini: typis J. Brindley, 1744, verso of the last leaf. Sir Joseph Banks's copy, now in the British Library, has its pages ruled with red lines.
16. *The Book Collector*, 2, 1953, p.253.
17. Anthony Hobson, *Great Libraries*, 1970, p.304.
18. Howard M. Nixon, *Twelve books in fine bindings from the library of J.W. Hely-Hutchinson*, Roxburghe Club, 1953, p.70.
19. Letter of 27 May 1629, quoted in W.D. Macray, *Annals of the Bodleian Library, Oxford*, 2nd edition, Oxford, 1890, p.69.
20. Letter of 2 February 1815 quoted in C.W. James, 'Some notes upon the manuscript library at Holkham', in *Library*, 4th ser, 2, 1922, p.233.
21. *The diary of Humphrey Wanley, 1715-1726*, ed. C.E. Wright and Ruth C. Wright, 2 vols, Bibliographical Society, 1966.
22. *Bibliographical Decameron*, 1817, II, p.451.
23. *The Enemies of Books*, Elliot Stock, 1902, p.29. Dr Katherine Swift observed in discussion that some of the Harleian books had not been pulled and re-sewn, but simply recovered, apparently to avoid the need to recut the edges.

24. *Diary of Humphrey Wanley*, II, p.395, 22 November 1725.
25. H.M. Nixon, *Twelve books*, pp.32-3, 36-47.
26. H.M. Nixon, *Broxbourne Library, styles and designs of bookbindings from the twelfth to the twentieth century*, 1956, pp.64-6.
27. Bodleian Library, Eng.lett.e.369, ff.82-95.
28. Transcript in Bodleian Library, MS Pollard 279 f.71.
29. *Gentleman's Magazine*, April 1745, 'State of periodical publications at London'.
30. After 1811 or 1812 in buff wrappers.
31. *The Library*, 5th ser. 9, 1956, pp.71-94
32. Pepys's *Diary*, 13 August 1666.
33. British Library, Jaffray papers, J2 f.62.
34. Stationers' Company archives, papers of John Kelly & Sons, box of miscellaneous material.
35. British Library, Add.MS 28275 f.382. The bookbinder Strap appears in *Roderick Random*.
36. Stationers' Company archives, Kelly papers, miscellaneous box.
37. Charles Ramsden, *Bookbinders of the United Kingdom (outside London) 1780-1840*, 1954.
38. First report of the commission for inquiring into the condition of the poorer classes in Ireland.
39. Eiluned Rees, 'Bookbinding in 18th century Wales' in *The Journal of the Welsh Bibliographical Society*, 12, 1983-4, pp.59-60.
40. Cadell & Davies, in reply to an enquiry from their printer, asked for 500 copies of a book to be sent in two separate lots. *The publishing firm of Cadell & Davies*, ed. Theodore Besterman, Oxford, 1938; letter from Peacock of 21 November 1808 and Cadell's reply.
41. Broadsheet giving postal rates in force from 18 January 1652, Guildhall Library, London.
42. Gibbon, *Letters* no.620.
43. Letter of 27 May 1629, quoted in W.D. Macray, *Annals*, p.69.
44. Wanley, *Diary*, entries for 27 June, 13 July 1721 (*Codex Aureus*); 29 October, 1 November 1720; 1, 2, 3 December 1724 (working at Wimpole).
45. W.P. Hassall. 'Thomas Coke, Earl of Leicester, 1697-1759' in *The Book Collector*, vol.8, no.3, 1959, pp.255-6.
46. Charles Ramsden, 'Richard Weir and Count MacCarthy-Reagh' in *The Book Collector*, vol.11, 1953, pp.247-57.
47. Howard M. Nixon, *Five centuries of English bookbinding*, Scolar Press, 1978, p.53.
48. John Evelyn, *Memoires for my Grandson*, Oxford for the Nonesuch Press, 1926, pp.51-52.
49. An exact account of the making of marbled paper by Mr. Evelin. British Library, MS Sloane 243, ff.96-98, reprinted in Charles Adams, 'Some notes on the art of marbling paper in the seventeenth century' in *Bulletin of the New York Public Library*, vol.51, no.7, July 1947, pp.417-420.
50. William Horman owned books bound by the Winchester binder whom Dr Neil Ker nicknamed The Virgin and Child Binder. It would appear that the tools mentioned in the will were those used by another binder who worked for the Eton College Library. See N.R. Ker 'The Virgin & Child Binder, LVL and William Horman', *The Library*, 5th series 17, 1962, pp.77-85; A.G. Watson, ed. *Books, Collections and Libraries*, 1985, pp.100-10.
51. Eiluned Rees, 'Bookbinding in 18th century Wales', in *The Journal of the Welsh Bibliographical Society*, vol.12, 1983-4, p.59.
52. Letter of 18 October, 1670, quoted in W. Salt Brassington, *A history of the art of*

bookbinding, 1894, p.222.

53. Evelyn, *Instructions*, p.84. This must surely be a very early use of the word 'conservation' in this sense.

54. Evelyn, *Instructions*, pp.46, 78.

55. *The Bodleian Library Account Book 1613-1646*, ed. Gwen Hampshire, Oxford, 1983, pp.80, 89, 93, 97, 101, 106.

56. British Library, Add. MS 34715, ff.3, 5, 6, 11.

57. The injunction 'to be bound like pattern volume 2' in the Kelly instructions quoted on p.33 implies a similar system.

58. This analysis is based on the 226 volumes with a John Evelyn provenance included in the first two days, 22 and 23 June 1977 of the sale at Christie's.

VI ET VIRTVTE

Fig. 1

Gentlemen and their book-plates

BRIAN NORTH LEE

THOMAS GORE of Alderton, whom John Aubrey in a 1671 letter called 'My stiffe starcht friend T.G., Cuckold & Esq.',[1] was too finicky, self-important and unusual to guide us on book-plate usage by gentlemen of his time. In his copious will,[2] however, he details:

A Plate of copper wherein is engraven my atchievement containing my coat Armour well marshalled...and Two more Copper plates containing...my Quarterings...and foure other copper plates of several sizes containing my Paternall Coate with Crest and Motto, which I desire also may be transmitted to Posterity. As also two other plates of copper in one of which is my Paternal Coate of Arms engraven in the midst with many faire flourishings at each end for Prints to be placed on the Top of Epistles dedicatory in Books. In the other is only engraven a Basket of Fruite and Flowers, for Prints to be set at the end of Books (below the Finis) for ornaments sake. As also my Paternall coate of Arms environ'd with Laurell engraven in Brass and set in Wood for a stamp to make an impression on the Covers of Books.[3] (See fig.1)

It totals nine coppers and a book stamp, and his will is dated 20 July 1683. His finest and first-named plate was by William Faithorne the elder.[4] There are five ex-libris and two book stamps recorded for Samuel Pepys;[5] and Sir Philip Sydenham, who became 3rd Baronet in 1696 and died in 1739, used eleven book-plates of which 23 varieties are known.[6] The first are dated 1699, and his bookpile is one of the first three examples in the style, devised by none other than Pepys (fig.2). Arthur Charlett, Master of University College, Oxford, in 1698 asked Pepys to make a cypher of his initials and suggest a motto for his ex-libris, and so, as related in the *Bodleian Library Record*,[7] 'Pepys was responsible for the chief features of the bookplate...a rectangular pile of books in three tiers, each row resting on books laid horizontally'. Surely either Charlett or Pepys showed Sydenham the design, for within a year he had Charlett's composition copied for himself. The only other 1699 bookpile was, understandably, for William Hewer, Pepys's secretary and friend.[8]

43

44

Fig. 2

The majority of gentlemen settled for a single book-plate, except where
it was desired to indicate ennoblement or new dignity; and no one matched
Sydenham's prolificity until it was belittled by the Victorian Sir William
Stirling-Maxwell, 9th Baronet,[9] 131 of whose plates are in the British
Museum Franks Collection (nor has he since been equalled in Britain).
Ornament and emblems being of absorbing interest to him, clearly the
designing of personal ex-libris was an attractive pastime (fig.3). Despite
general satisfaction with a single book-plate, it is surprising how many occur
in varieties of state, with motto, arms or design amended or the engraver's
signature erased; and the occasional somewhat slavish copying of an
individual's book-plate was probably due to the original copper's being lost.
Until the late 1800s most book-plates were the work of trade engravers,
called on for serviceable compositions, so few ex-libris are outstanding
engravings. The possession of a library, desire for identity, or response to
stylistic fashion encouraged many sons to have their own book-plates, but as
a cheap alternative inscriptions could be changed or scissors brought into
service. One of a series of book-plates by the engraver of Blome's *Gwillim,*
1679,[10] illustrates the latter alternative (fig.4). Doubtless used by Sir Thomas
Windsor Hunloke, 3rd Baronet,[11] who succeeded his father in 1715, he
simply cut off the inscription, which read: 'Sr. Henry Hunloke of Winger-
worth in Derbyshire Bart. In ye Escotcheon of pretence is ye Armes of

Fig. 3

Fig. 4

Katherine his Lady, who was sole daughter & heyre of Francis Tyrwhit of Kettleby in Lincolnshire Esqr ye last of ye Eldest branch of ye great & antient family.' Heraldically, of course, Sir Thomas should have quartered his mother's arms, not kept them in pretence, but the copper or unused prints would be at hand, so why not use them?

Book-plate history will always be incomplete, partly due to the removal of ex-libris from books in the heady days of collecting, 1880 to 1910. The

Fig. 5

carelessness or inadequacy of engravers or their commissioners in detailing arms, or deliberate use of unentitled arms, often inhibit ascription, as does use of just the paternal coat when an impalement would have been in order. Mere plates for books were not high amongst most gentlemen's priorities. An anonymous and unambitious woodcut armorial in Franks serves as instance (fig.5). Cadwallader impaling Pelsant are there questioned as the arms, being badly done; but the plate belonged to the Rev. Arthur Collier, and is printed on the verso of the half-title of a memoir of him by Robert Benson.[12] Benson tells us, incidentally, that Collier died in embarrassed circumstances, and that 'such portions of his effects as his relatives deemed it indelicate to sell' were sent to relatives. Among them he lists a drinking-glass and the wood block of his arms. It was a gentlemanly consideration.

These details indicate that personal whim furthered early book-plate usage in Britain and that ex-libris could be valued possessions; but (excepting collegiate book labels, which were printed and not engraved) ex-libris were so rarely used that they were a minimal part of the output of any engraving shops until *c.*1700. Three plates are known of the 16th century, and upwards of 200 in the next, mostly made in its last quarter and as yet inadequately researched. Two of the former and some of the latter were not ex-libris *per se*, but adapted, mostly after serving as illustration or ornament in books. Our earliest plate, for Sir Nicholas Bacon's gift of books to Cambridge University, uses a woodcut from Leigh's *Accedence of Armory*.[13] Ex-libris of John Marsham, of Kent, as esquire and baronet, illustrated title-

Fig. 6

pages as well,[14] as no doubt did others (fig.6). The modest but dignified Ent armorial long puzzled collectors. Its incorrect, single arms[15] are unhelpful, and Franks questioned the attribution. G.H. Viner suggested it was David Loggan's work, based on a design by Michel le Blon,[16] its tassels and double serifs like those on Sir Thomas Isham's plate, documented as Loggan's work. Anthony Pincott, however, found it printed on the verso of the title-page of Ent's *Laureae Apollinari*, Padua, 1636. It was thus decades earlier than Loggan, and served in a book. Sir George Ent,[17] a medical man and original fellow of the Royal Society, was son of a merchant from the Low Countries; and his book-plate is still found in books, including P. Heylin's *A Help to English History*, 1672, in the Society of Antiquaries' library. The *Dictionary of National Biography* actually details his arms in the above-mentioned book of poems, so it is surprising that the book-plate was not identified long ago.

Not surprisingly, however, few book-plate users actually designated themselves 'Gentleman' (abbreviated to 'Gent.') in their book-plate inscriptions, though one recalls a dozen who did in the 18th century, including John Gore of London (fig.7). One feels the designation should be

Fig. 7

implicit, unlike 'esquire', proper on book-plates (but rarely elsewhere) in indicating right to bear arms below knightly rank. In preparing this address 'gentleman' posed questions. Good birth and social standing (technically above yeoman status) are implied, and in some usages the nobility. Honourable and refined, by modern understanding of the term, gentlemen were also somewhat leisured, and it follows that the best of them had time

50

Fig. 8

for books. Gore's Jacobean plate is one of the finest in the style. James Bengough, Gent., declares himself on his Early Armorial plate (fig.8) to be of Inner Temple in 1702, and he is named in the 1705 records, but there is no evidence he was called to the bar.[18] More significant here is that his book-plate was from William Jackson's workshop near the Inns of Court. Jackson, who clearly employed several engravers, produced over 600 book-plates between 1695 and 1715, and was thus the prime populariser of book-plate usage in Britain. His pattern book, called the 'Brighton Collection' (on account of its having been found there in the last century), is in the British Museum. What has it to tell us?

It was not assembled early in his career, for many of the plates are grubby, and there is some duplication among its 640 examples. Jackson impressively promoted use of book-plates in two sizes, for large and small books – a good idea which never caught on significantly. The Duke of Beaufort's plates[19] are an instance, the smaller being about 3¼ inches high (fig.9). In Cambridge and then Oxford, 1700-1704, he acquired orders for college ex-libris, supplying coppers and prints and undertaking the arduous

F. 27572 & #9

Fig. 9

S.ʳ Godfry Kneller K.ᵗ Principall
Painter to his Majesty : 1701

Fig. 10

pasting of plates into books. Though institutional plates are outside our brief
a point they evidence must be mentioned: existence in the 'Brighton' book
of otherwise unknown armorials for Balliol, Wadham and Oriel Colleges
(All Souls bought a copper from Jackson but never used it) strongly implies
that he engraved the plates before offering them. This view is supported by
the book-plates of individuals which were evidently not used, Sir Godfrey
Kneller's (fig.10) and John Evelyn's being instances. Most likely they were
approached but turned his offer down. Jackson was but one of many able
trade engravers in London, and it is inconceivable that (at a rough count)
about 100 of the nobility (including 14 dukes), over 60 baronets, about 30
knights and over 250 gentry and others just gravitated to him for ex-libris.
He simply must have sought them out.[20]

Jackson, and others of his time, worked concurrently from 1700 in the
Early Armorial style, which we have seen, and the Jacobean, represented
by the plate of Mrs Margaret Massingberd, showing the two Massingberd
coats quarterly. Burrell Massingberd preferred an Early Armorial, and the
two are a modest example of the marked employment of Jackson by some
families. (fig.11). The Brownlowes of Belton, Lincolnshire, had eight book-

Burrell Massingberd of South
Ormesbye in Com. Lincolne Esq.

Mrs Margret Massingberd
1704

Fig. 11

Fig. 12

plates from the workshop, and one for Dame Dorothy's mother, Dame Anna Margaretta Mason, makes a ninth. The Berties had seven; there are nine Cecil ex-libris; and numerous families were clients for several plates. It is evidence that the idea of an ex-libris for one's books was becoming attractive in the 1700-1715 period.

Since few book-plate makers signed their work, and when they did, but part of it, we have limited knowledge of the extent of local commissioning, but towns had their engravers; Cambridge, for instance, had William Stephens in the century's middle years. The Chippendale armorial was by then fashionable, and his ex-libris for Samuel Kerrich (fig.12), though modest, is of note in that documentation about its making survives.[21] Stephens charged 12*s* for the copper and 10*s* 6*d* for 800 prints on 16 September 1754, and adds: 'I have done but 800 because you seem'd in doubt whether you shou'd want quite 1000 at present; if you have any further Commands, shall take great care to please'. Had more orders or bills survived we should have a clearer idea of the extent of gentlemen's libraries in the 17th and 18th centuries.

Three-quarters of a century earlier the engraver David Loggan made a gift to Sir Thomas Isham, who was still just in his teens (fig.13). He wrote to Isham on 8 January 1676: 'Sr, I send yow hier a Print of your cote of arms. I have Printet 200 wich I will send with the plate...as a small Niewe Yaers gieft or a acknowledgement in part for all your favours, if any thing in it be amiss I shall be glad to mind it. I have taken the Heralds painters derection in it, it is werry much used a mongst persons of Quality to past

OSTENDO NON OSTENTO

On things transitory, resteth no glory.

Fig. 13

ther Cotes of Armes before ther Bookes in stade of Wreithing ther names'.[22] Does the number printed perhaps indicate the size of many orders of the time? We lack, incidentally, evidence that as many persons of quality then were so much given to book-plate usage as Loggan suggests; but the tone of ingratiation from both Loggan and Stephens is marked. They kept their place in communicating with the gentry.

A minority of gentlemen opted for pictorial-armorial or pictorial plates, and a nice example for Sir John Henniker, 1st Baronet, includes castle and

Fig. 14

landscape in a shipping scene, with an anchor (fig.14). The latter components were perhaps especially apt, for he was the son of John Henniker, a London merchant. Married at St Paul's Cathedral in 1747 to Anne, eldest daughter and co-heir of Sir John Major, Baronet, he became a baronet himself in 1765 and died in 1800. The question of gentlemanly definition becomes tedious in the niceties of qualification; but suffice it to say that, as the baronetage was instituted to raise money,[23] early creations were notable county landowners. Some had acquired wealth through trade, and many of their descendants became peers; but later, as Hugh Montgomery-Massingberd observes in his fine introduction to the 1983 edition of Cokayne's *Complete Baronetage*, neither land nor endowment were required. Professional success itself could be so honoured.

Allegorical pictorials, often with arms, predated landscapes in popularity, and both have continued in varying guise. Cherubs, or *amorini*, were a feature, and were sometimes seen disporting themselves amongst books in libraries. Two plates, from the same copper, of Joshua Scrope, for his residences at Cockerington and Long Sutton, Lincolnshire, are signed 'C & A. Paas Sculpt. No.53 Holborn' (fig.15). They were probably made between 1788 and 1793,[24] and there is said to be a third variety which I have not seen.[25] Though a charming composition, the cherubs, if responsible for the unhappy litter of books and inkwells at base, would have quickly been banished from the library, provided the one bearing the oval's weight survived long enough.

Fig. 15

A book-plate with identical design, but a greek key border, for Charles Hoare[26] may also have been Paas's work (fig.16); and Charles's family is probably unequalled in the number of fine and diverse ex-libris which they used in a little over a hundred years. The plates are also an instance of social mobility. Henry Hoare, of Walton in Buckinghamshire, was a yeoman farmer. His son Henry (*d.*1668), of St. Botolph's, Aldersgate, was a yeoman and dealer in horses at Smithfield (and, according to a kinsman, made as much as 'four hundred poundes a year which in those days was a considerable somme'). His son, Sir Richard Hoare, Knight, banker and goldsmith (*d.*1718), became Lord Mayor of London, and from the outset of his business kept 'running cashes', the equivalent of today's banking accounts. In 1690 he moved to Fleet Street, and Hoare's Bank, which kept his sign of the Golden Bottle, has been at the same premises (No.37) ever since.

Fig. 16

Of five sons and a daughter of his 17 children who lived to maturity, two sons – Benjamin and Henry – had book-plates. Henry, his father's partner from 1702, calls himself 'Goldsmith in London 1704' on his book-plate (fig.17). Both brothers' Jacobean ex-libris may have been the work of gold and silver engravers, and are individual in character. Henry bought Stourton Castle and its estates in 1720, and changed the name to Stourhead. His memorial in the church there reads: 'His character is too great to be described, and yet too good to be concealed. His love of God and mankind were so ardent that he sought all opportunity of honouring the one and doing

59

Fig. 17

good to the other. He was strictly pious himself, without being censorious of others; truly humble without affectation; grave without moroseness, cheerful without levity; just beyond exception, and merciful without reserve'. Not just a gentleman, then, but a paragon! Numerous varieties exist of an armorial gift plate for his bequest of books for furthering faith and piety (fig. 18). The inscription is self-explanatory.

His elder son, Henry, 19 years old at his father's death, inherited the banking business and Stourhead on his majority. He landscaped the gardens, brought in temples and statuary, and filled his house with treasures. Two book-plates ascribed to him differ in the heads at base, and though otherwise identical are of separate engraving (fig. 19); so perhaps the second was made as a result of the original copper's having been lost. Henry's brother Richard was knighted, and Richard's son was created a baronet. Sir Richard Colt Hoare, 2nd Baronet, was his son. I have elsewhere[27] given an account of the book-plates of the family and its connections, notably the Aclands. Between them, allowing for varieties of state, there are over 30 ex-libris, some of them very fine pictorial-armorials. There is neither space nor need to detail

60

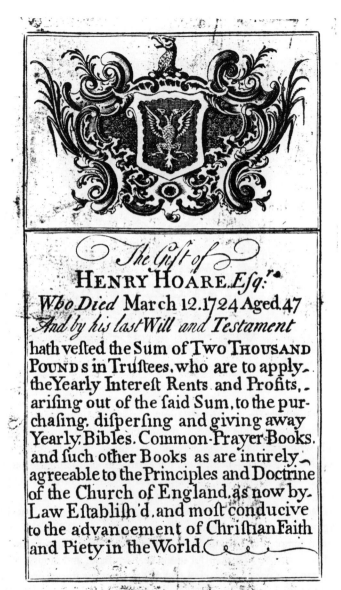

The Gift of
HENRY HOARE. *Esq.*
Who Died March 12. 1724 Aged 47
And by his last Will and Testament
hath vefted the Sum of Two THOUSAND
POUND s in Truftees, who are to apply
the Yearly Intereft Rents and Profits,
arifing out of the faid Sum, to the pur-
chafing, difperfing and giving away
Yearly, Bibles, Common-Prayer Books,
and fuch other Books as are intirely
agreeable to the Principles and Doctrine
of the Church of England, as now by
Law Eftablifh'd, and moft conducive
to the advancement of Chriftian Faith
and Piety in the World.

Fig. 18

them here, but illustration of two will demonstrate their quality and interest
(figs. 20 and 21).

It would be as wrong to assume that individuals and families who did
not use ex-libris did not love books as it would be to believe that use of

Henry Hoare

Henry Hoare

Fig. 19

Fig. 20

Fig. 21

Fig. 22

book-plates implies bibliophily. The book-plate may be seen merely as an adjunct of gentlemanly style, in the same way that a room in the country or town residence enjoys the designation 'library'. Whether it is actively used is quite another matter. It is also too simplistic to view the book-plate as the natural mark of ownership for people of substance and its humbler counterpart, the printed or engraved book label, as the alternative used by lesser folk. A delightfully broad spectrum of trade and society used book labels.[28] I have long observed the wide recourse to book labels amongst East Anglian residents, for instance; and generally the choice may have been due to taste or custom. Sir Francis Skipwith, of Newbold Revel in Warwickshire, used a simple typographic label with printer's ornament border during his Baronetcy, 1728-78 (fig.22). His father, by contrast, used handsome armorials in two sizes by William Jackson, comparable to the Duke of Somerset's book-plates, already illustrated.

The now rather mocked 'Lady Bountiful' syndrome has relevance to our subject, for gentility – male or female – has been seen to impose responsibilities not only to servants and retainers but to the poor. As illustration the Acland bequest plate can serve a dual purpose (fig.23). Dated 1844 it records a bequest of £1,000, the interest to be spent on Bibles and Common Prayer books for the Devonshire poor and especially those in parishes where Acland had property. The plate's additional interest will be evident to you, for it is clearly based on Henry Hoare's bequest plate, but in contemporary style. Acland died unmarried (Burke's *Peerage and Baronetage* states in 1843, but the book label is probably right); his sister was married to Sir Henry Hugh Hoare, 3rd Baronet, whose mother was Frances Ann Acland

64

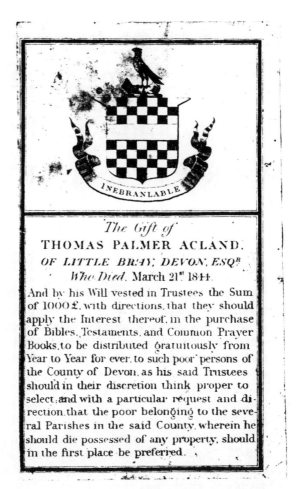

Fig. 23

before her marriage to Sir Richard Hoare, 1st Baronet. Book-plates not infrequently beget – or at least inspire – others.

Few servants' library plates are recorded, but a simple 1906 label (fig.24) records Miss Ewald's last gift to the servants' hall library at Cave Castle. Prince Leopold used one, and probably Queen Victoria for the staff at Windsor and also Balmoral – but Royal circles lie beyond our brief. In the wider context of encouragement of inferiors to virtue, one would have liked to illustrate a handsome label with crest, motto and the text: 'This Book was given by R. & T. Orford to [Elizabeth Broadhurst, she] having from a sense of duty to God, and to avoid a temptation, not been in any Public House

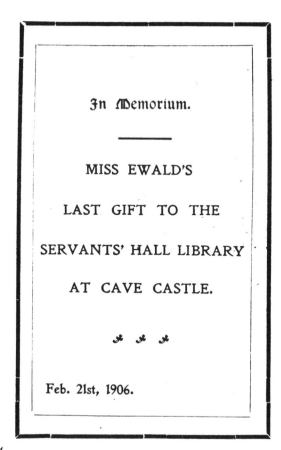

In Memorium.

———

MISS EWALD'S

LAST GIFT TO THE

SERVANTS' HALL LIBRARY

AT CAVE CASTLE.

⚘ ⚘ ⚘

Feb. 21st, 1906.

Fig. 24

during Disley Wakes, in November 18[57?].' There was a print of it in the collection of the late Sir Harry Page, of Manchester.[29]

The Jacobean book-plate of John Newsham, who married Anne, the daughter and co-heir of the Rt. Hon. James Craggs, is an early instance of the occasional incorporation of 'No.', though here as quite often no number has been inserted (fig.25). It brings us to the question of shelf-marks. Much less than half of 1% of book-plate users seem to have bothered with shelf-marks.[30] Other manuscript additions are very uncommon, but have included the volume's title, place of residence or the holding of an incumbency, and donatory inscriptions. The Jacobean plate of Beaupré Bell (1704-45) has 'donum' added in manuscript (fig.26). An antiquary, Bell was especially interested in ancient coins; his father had squandered the family money, but

Fig. 25

with £1,500 a year Beaupré could gratify his tastes. Stylistically the book-plate could have been his father's, but the arms are Bell quartering Oldfield (his mother's family), so the ownership is in no doubt. Another occasional addition to book-plates was contemporary hand-colouring, which occurs on another print of Bell's ex-libris. Its fuller manuscript inscriptions refer to his membership of the Peterborough Literary Club,[31] his M.A., and his donation of the book. Bell, who also belonged to the Spalding Gentlemen's Society, died of consumption on the road to Bath and left his books, etc., to his old college, Trinity, at Cambridge.

In the 18th century the Chippendale period, *c*.1740-75, was the most prolific for book-plate production, and the spade shield armorials of its last quarter are – a little surprisingly – less numerous. Throughout most of the 19th century the so-called 'die-sinker' armorial predominated; and during this time nearly anyone who was or fancied himself a gentleman would have at least one ex-libris. The Rev. John Skinner was the son of Russell Skinner, a Hertfordshire gentleman (fig.27). He would visit Stourhead to talk antiquities with Sir Richard Colt Hoare, and mixed in society, but in his

Fig. 26

parish, Camerton, and the locality he saw vice everywhere. He compared the lady of the manor with Jezebel and Catherine of Russia, believed every cottage a brothel, saw ill in most people, and blamed Winchester (where his sons were educated) for their rebelliousness. He wrote in his Journal on Sunday 27 June 1830: 'I had to marry a couple at half-past eight; the bride was as round as a barrel and according to custom, I suppose there will be a christening in the course of the honeymoon'. In the end poor Skinner's

68

IOANNES SKINNER A.M.

Fig. 27   CAMERTON.

fancies overwhelmed him, he took a pistol, and shot himself. He was, nevertheless, a gentleman.[32]

Another unhappy parson, unhappy for a different reason, was the Rev. William Dodd. He used a crest plate in two varieties, one having 'Chaplain to the King' added (fig.28).[33] His motto was 'wise and harmless', but wise he certainly was not, and its companion is in question. There is an intriguing account of him in the *Dictionary of National Biography*. The son of a clergyman, he married a wife whose 'reputation was perhaps doubtful'; he was an author and a poet, but scandals accrued to him, not least financial ones. Ultimately he was arrested for forgery of a bond. Attempts, including those of Dr Johnson, to have him pardoned were to no avail, so he was hanged on 27 June 1777. It was said he spoke to the hangman about ways of preventing death, but when his body was brought down the crush of people made any hope of resuscitation impossible. It was, incidentally, to Dodd that Dr Johnson referred in commenting: 'Depend upon it, Sir, when a man knows that he is to be hanged in a fortnight, it concentrates his mind wonderfully'.

W. Dodd. M.A.

Fig. 28

W. Dodd. M.A.
Chaplain to the King.

Fig. 29

'Gentleman' is variously defined in diverse contexts. Boutell's *Heraldry*,[34] for instance, understands it to mean, 'In heraldry, the lowest rank of armigerous persons'. All men possessed of armorial ex-libris are thus gentlemen, but only – and there's the rub – if they are entitled to the arms they portray. The novelist Charles Dickens used a crest on his ex-libris and his silver plate originally granted by the College of Arms to William Dickens in 1625, to which he had no hereditary or lawful claim (fig.29).[35] The question is, however, somewhat complicated overall. Not all using unentitled arms were deliberately cheating: the engraver or herald adviser may have made a mistake; there may have been an oral family tradition concerning lineage honestly believed in; or published heraldic works may have been misleading, deliberately or unintentionally. Not until the 19th century did genealogy become widely authoritative and scholarly. As Hugh Montgomery-Massingberd has observed, the previous century was 'the golden age of bad genealogy',[36] and it abounded in romantic nonsense for the benefit of the pretentious. Book-plates are also a special problem on account of their small size and the not infrequent inability of engravers to create unambiguous depictions.

Dr R. Glynn Clobery used three book-plates (fig.30). His Jacobean – very late stylistically – cannot be earlier than 1758, when he became M.D. The arms are Gules three harpoons points downwards argent. His subsequent Chippendale plate is of much superior engraving, but one sees that Glynn has adopted a different motto and added the surname Clobery, he having inherited Clobery property. A Fellow of the Royal College of Physicians, a scholar, and friend of the poet Gray (whom he attended in his last illness), he was eccentric but benevolent,[37] and died aged over 80 in 1800, apparently of a cold caught visiting the damp depository of the Rowleian MSS. Was his third book-plate made because the Chippendale copper was lost, because he wanted a contemporary spade shield, or because of the arms? The last seems most probable, and the lamentable engraving may be dated 1790, for it is

Fig. 30

probably of this that he wrote in a letter of 6 May that year: 'Dear Sir, Damn all taste! say I: whether at Cambridge, or in St Paul's church yard: whether at Liddiard's shop, or Dr Peckard's[38] – I wish the arms had been done agreably to ye drawing: but since matters wd not be right, we must be contented; 'tis most assuredly, not worth while to have it altered, or to be at any further trouble abt it'. He has replaced his paternal Glynn arms with those of Clobery. Without Burke's *General Armory* at hand, however, it would be difficult to guess the arms. Argent a chevron (apparently sable) between three...what? They are actually meant to be bats.[39]

72

Sir Tho: Brand Kn.^t
Gentleman Usher of the Green Rod,
and Gentleman Usher Daily Wait^r
to His Majesty. Anno 17 35.

Fig. 31

Finally, there are a handful of ex-libris of those who are gentlemen by
title. Sir Thomas Brand's plate is an instance (fig.31). As its inscription tells,
he was 'Gentleman Usher of the Green Rod and Gentleman Usher Daily
Waitr to His Majesty' in 1735. There are several variants, detailed
elsewhere,[40] but Sir Thomas had not been in a hurry to have a book-plate,
for he held the same post under King George I. Several of the Corps of
Gentlemen-at-Arms have also used book-plates. It seemed slightly odd to see
the Countess of Oxford and Mortimer's plate (fig.32) illustrating the
brochure for this conference; but gentlemen's spouses are ladies, and they
should have had place here had space allowed. Henrietta Cavendish Holles
Harley, Countess of Oxford and Mortimer, has special claim to inclusion,
anyway, in view of the percentage of her large fortune which her husband
spent in enhancing his father's library. To gentlemen who knew how to
spend money and loved books, Hannah Glasse, had she written 'The Art of

Henrietta Cavendish Holles
Oxford and Mortimer
Given me by my Lord June 1732

Fig. 32

the Bibliophile' instead of *The Art of Cookery*, might have cautioned 'First catch your heiress'.

The Oxford and Mortimer book-plate was engraved by George Vertue.[41] Equally impressive, but different in character, is Samuel Wale's ex-libris for Henrietta Louisa Fermor, Countess of Pomfret – one of three she possessed. The most handsome, it names her post as 'Lady of the Bed-chamber to Queen Caroline'. A grand-daughter of Judge Jeffreys, who though a gentleman was not gentlemanly, she was much mocked for essaying to learnedness. Walpole laughed at her 'paltry air of significant learning and absurdity', and noted her total lack of humour.[42] She died in 1761 on the road to Bath (was it littered with expired nobility and gentlefolk?) Presumably her several other book-plates played their part in her pretension to scholarship. In the other ex-libris discussed we have seen pretence to lineage, pride in distinction, artistic taste (and the lack of it), ambition and modesty, and remarkable individuality. Book-plates, with all their inadequacies and the questions they leave unanswered, are the most useful leads we have to the history of bibliophily in this country – and the book-plates of gentlemen form a major part of that story.

References

1. See Anthony Powell's *John Aubrey and his friends*, 1948, for an account of the vicissitudes of his relationship with Thomas Gore (1632-84).
2. The full passage relating to the coppers is quoted in *The Ex Libris Journal*, Vol.13, 1903, p.117. The will is printed in full in 'The Last Will of Thomas Gore, the Antiquary', by the Rev. Canon J.E. Jackson, FSA (*Wiltshire Archaeological Magazine*, XIV, 1873).
3. See the writer's *British Bookplates*, 1979, p.30, No.13, for comment on the armorials. Five of the Gore plates, with a duplicate and a copy, are in the Franks Collection (F.12321-12325). Examples in the Henderson Smith Collection at the National Library of Scotland, Edinburgh, include the arms 'with faire flourishings' and the basket of fruit and flowers.
4   The elder William Faithorne (1616-91) engraved four other book-plates: a large armorial, probably for Sir George Hungerford of Cadenham; large and small armorials for the Mariots of Whitchurch; and a portrait plate recording the bequest of books by John Hacket, Bishop of Lichfield and Coventry, to Cambridge University Library.
5. See *British Bookplates*, 1979, p.28, Nos.11 & 12; *The Ex Libris Journal*, Vol.3, 1893, pp.165-169; *ibid*. Vol.4, 1894, p.105; and Cyril Davenport's *English Heraldic Book-Stamps*, 1909, pp.308-311.
6. See F.J. Thairlwall's article, 'Men of many bookplates', in *The Ex Libris Journal*, Vol.9, 1899, pp.157-161,and Carnegy Johnson's article, 'Book-plates of Sir Philip Sydenham', *ibid*, Vol.12, 1902, pp.5-8.
7. Vol.2, No.17, December 1941, p.23.
8. See *The Ex Libris Journal*, Vol.11, 1901, pp.152-153, pp.164-169, and Vol.12, 1902, pp.9-10,
9. (1818-78). Scolar Press in 1988 published David Weston's *A Short Title Catalogue of the Emblem Books and Related Works in the Stirling Maxwell Collection of Glasgow University Library*.
10. Others in the series were for Sir John Berkenhead, Walter Chetwynd, Randolph Egerton, Justinian Pagit, Samuel Pepys, Charles Pitfeild, Sir Robert Southwell and William Wharton.
11. (1684-1752).
12. *Robert Benson, Memoirs of the life and writings of the Rev. Arthur Collier*, 1837.
13. The woodcut first appeared in the second edition, 1568, replacing the arms of the first edition (Bacon having in the meantime received a new grant of arms from the College of Heralds). It was then used for the book-plate, and subsequently in four later editions of the

book; but even at the third edition's printing, in 1576, further wear to the block is evident, and this is even more marked later.

14. F.19825, Marsham's plate as esquire, was also used on the title-page of *Diatriba Chronologica*, 1649. F.19825, his plate as baronet, occurs on the title of *Chronicus Canon Aegyptiacus Ebraicus Graecus & Disquisitiones D. Johannis Marshami Eq. Aur & Bar.*, London, 1672. (The latter is easily distinguished from the title-page cut since it has wide margins and lacks 'Aristoteles' printed on the back).

15. Before identification, it was questioned whether this anonymous armorial related to Ent(e), Bell or Skene on the evidence of its arms. Debate is now, of course, irrelevant; but both Papworth and Burke indicate that the field should be azure not sable.

16. Viner noted in Dr Strohl's *Heraldischer Atlas* a page of some 15 facsimile reproductions of early mantled shields with helms (without arms and crests). The first ten were by Theodore de Bry; 11-15 were attributed to Michel le Blon (c.1590-1656) and had affinity to two of the Loggan plates. They also occur in Fox-Davies's *The Art of Heraldry*, the illustrations on p.cix and the information concerning them on pp.434-5. See also 'Bookplates engraved by David Loggan', by the late G.H. Viner, *The Bookplate Society Newsletter* No.4, October 1974, pp.2-6.

17. (1604-89).

18. See 'The bookplates of Serjeants at Law' by J.H. Baker, *The Bookplate Journal*. Volume 3, Number 2, September 1985, p.67.

19. Henry, 2nd Duke of Beaufort (1684-1714) married in 1706, as his second wife, Rachel, daughter and co-heir of Baptist, Earl of Gainsborough. It is interesting to note that the 1706 book-plate was engraved for the Duchess, and amended in its inscription for the Duke.

20. For an account of Jackson and his book-plates see 'Oxford bookplates by William Jackson – new light on the Brighton Collection', by Anthony Pincott, *The Bookplate Society Newsletter*, No.6, June 1974, pp.3-10.

21. See *The Ex Libris Journal*, Vol.3, 1893, pp.10-12.

22. See 'The correspondence of David Loggan with Sir Thomas Isham' by Sir Gyles Isham, Bart., in *The Connoisseur*, April and October 1963.

23. See Hugh Montgomery-Massingberd's introduction to G.E. Cokayne's *Complete Baronetage*, Alan Sutton, Gloucester, 1983.

24. See Ian Maxted, *The London Book Trades 1775-1800*, Dawson, 1977. This address is given for Paas 1788-1809, but they traded as C. & A. Paas 1785-93 (and were described as Charles and Andrew in 1785).

25. This fact is noted in *The Ex Libris Journal*, Vol.2, 1892, p.139; but there is no detailing of the differences.

26. (1767-1851). This book-plate is not earlier than 1790, in which year he married Frances Dorothea, elder daughter of Sir George Robinson, 5th Bart., of Cranford, Northants. It is in two states. The Crouch Collection print, shown, has a border; another in the Franks Collection (F.14854) lacks the border. See the writer's article 'Some bookplates of the Hoare family of Stourhead', *The Bookplate Society Newsletter*, Vol.2, No.22, June 1978, for fuller details of Charles Hoare's five ex-libris.

27. In the article referred to in footnote 26.

28. See the writer's *Early Printed Book Labels*, Private Libraries Association and the Bookplate Society, 1976; and 'Bookplates for all sorts and conditions of men', in the *Antiquarian Book Monthly Review*, Vol.II, No.8, Issue 18, August 1975.

29. Sir Harry Page's 300-volume collection of albums and commonplace books, is now lodged with the John Rylands University Library of Manchester. See *The Ephemerist* (Journal of

The Ephemera Society), No.68, March 1990.

30. Collectors and writers on book-plates scarcely ever take note of shelf-marks. Frequently, of course, such detailing would have been elsewhere than on the ex-libris, though 'No.' as part of the engraved composition was an encouragement to proper ordering of a library. Incorporation of a blank compartment, or two as on the book-plate of Sir Frederick Adam (1781-1853), sometime Governor of Madras, was an alternative. The antiquary Ralph Sheldon (1623-84) and George, Earl Macartney (1737-1806) are instances of bibliophiles who assiduously placed shelf-marks on their ex-libris.

31. The Spalding Gentlemen's Society is the most well-known provincial institution of its kind, and was 'a Society of Gentlemen for the supporting mutual benevolence, and their improvement in the Liberal Sciences and Polite Learning'. Its counterpart at Peterborough was founded by the Rev. Timothy Neve; it was formally affiliated to the Society of Antiquaries at a meeting on 14 November 1722; and its successor was the Peterborough Book Society. Charles Balguy (1708-67), sometime its secretary, used a bookpile ex-libris in five different colour printings (see 'Bookplates and bibliography', p.35, in Myers and Harris, *Publishing History Occasional Series 2, Bibliophily*, 1986). See Joan Evans, *A History of the Society of Antiquaries*, Oxford, 1956, pp.53-4.

32. See Virginia Woolf's essay on him in *The Common Reader* of 1932; *Journal of a Somerset Rector*, edited by H. & P. Coombs, Kingsmead Press, Bath, 1972; and the *Dictionary of National Biography*.

33. He was appointed Chaplain to the King in 1763 and held the post until 1774.

34. 1963 revised edition, Warne, London, p.286.

35. See 'Dickens and his "heraldic crest"', by T.P. Cooper, in *Dickensian*, October 1922, pp.194-6.

36. See 23.

37. See *The Ex Libris Journal*, Vol.2, 1892, pp.8-9.

38. Peter Peckard was Master of Magdalene College, Cambridge.

39. Bats are a very uncommon heraldic charge. Burke's *General Armory* gives the arms of Clobery, of Bradston, co. Devon as: Argent a chevron between three bats displayed sable.

40. See the writer's *London Bookplates*, The Bookplate Society and Forlaget Exlibristen 1985, p.133, No.268.

41. George Vertue (1684-1756) engraved five other ex-libris, listed in H.W. Fincham's *Artists and Engravers of British and American Book Plates*, London, 1897. The ex-libris illustrated here was described in Horace Walpole's *Catalogue of Engravers*, 1794, as a 'Plate to put in Lady Oxford's books'.

42. See *DNB*.

Was Henry Yates Thompson a Gentleman?

CHRISTOPHER DE HAMEL

THE ELUSIVE definition of a 'gentleman' has exercised the minds of drawing-room conversationalists for hundreds of years, but I now propose to give you the definitive answer of what constitutes a gentleman, at least in terms of Sotheby catalogues. A gentleman pays 10% commission. It is as simple as that; and there are no exceptions. Dealers, marchant-amateurs, friends of cousins, neighbours of the man whose son we were at school with, bullying real estate agents, book runners, former members of staff, and very many others may (in fact) very well end up paying trade terms of 6% or less, but if so, their lots are never designated in a book catalogue as 'The property of a gentleman'. For this privilege you pay full commission. If a dealer insists on being so described (and they do sometimes) we have a whole vocabulary of evasive alternative designations, such as 'The property of a collector' (that means trade, the implication being that a gentleman doesn't collect – he owns), 'The property of a trust' (that means they are trying to avoid tax as well as commission), 'The property of a continental consignor', 'Another property', and so on. But, to be accorded the designation of a gentleman, you pay gentleman's commission.

Let us then apply this test at once to Henry Yates Thompson. He was constantly selling books and manuscripts at Sotheby's, in particular in 12 sales totalling some 500 lots between 1899 and 1921, eight of them with single-owner catalogues.[1] In the first there is no designation at all: in fact the ambiguous implication is that the lots offered for sale belonged still to the estate of the aristocratic Lord Ashburnham from whose collection Yates Thompson had purchased them three years before. In the next two sales the books appear as 'The property of a well-known collector' (a subtle snub in Edwardian London but I expect that means 5 or 6%), then in 1903 (for perhaps he had objected) 'The property of a well-known amateur' and the same two years later, which means the same but sounds a little more leisured. Then at last in 1904 and 1912 there are his lots called 'The property of a gentleman', but only twice in 12 sales. In 1908 he is named: 'The property of H. Yates Thompson, Esq.', in 1914 'The property of Harry

Yates Thompson, Esq.' (too informal), and for the three monumentally great sales of 1919 to 1921, 'The property of Henry Yates Thompson', no Esquire. In fact, the letter survives from Sotheby's in October 1918 proposing the commission rate for these sales: 'in view of your long and friendly Association with us', wrote Montague Barlow (what he meant was that there was nothing he could do about it), Sotheby's accepted to sell the manuscripts for 5%.[2] Yates Thompson, in short, was not a gentleman consignor.

In all our modern connotations, Henry Yates Thompson was a gentleman through and through: 'born to wealth and position', as Josiah Bennett expressed it,[3] in 1838, the eldest son of a Liverpool banker. He was educated at Harrow, where he was head of school, and Trinity College Cambridge where he won the Porson Prize for Greek verse in 1860. He trained as a barrister and was called to the bar in 1867 but never practised. He contested three elections as a liberal candidate but failed to be elected to parliament, and instead spent much of his early middle years in idle travel in Europe, Egypt, the Holy Land, India, the West Indies, America, and so on. Mr H.P. Kraus once owned the journal that Yates Thompson had kept during the American Civil War during which he went out of his way to watch battles in progress. For five years from 1862, Yates Thompson was private secretary to Lord Spencer, Viceroy of Ireland. He was for a time editor of the *Pall Mall Gazette* but sold it in 1892 to the first Lord Astor. His portrait hangs in the reading room of the London Library. His house was no.19 Portman Square, coincidentally well-known to art historians because until recently it formed part of the Courtauld Institute. Here Yates Thompson kept his collections and gave enchanting dinner parties, presided over by his wife Elizabeth, whom he married in 1878. She was daughter and heiress of George Smith, founder and owner of the *Dictionary of National Biography*, which she inherited, and this fact perhaps ensured Yates Thompson a place in the *DNB*, for which Eric Millar wrote a charming entry after Yates Thompson's death in his ninetieth year on 8 July 1928.[4]

I should acknowledge three other secondary sources too before we proceed. The first is a handlist of Yates Thompson's medieval manuscripts compiled by Seymour de Ricci in 1926, neither entirely comprehensive nor of course up-to-date but a fascinating and very useful piece of antiquarian documentation.[5] The next is an extremely witty and diverting article written for *The Book Collector* in 1967 by Josiah Q. Bennett, based on Yates Thompson's correspondence with Sotheby's during the sales of 1919-21, now in the Lilly Library at Indiana, filled with anecdote and prices.[6] Anthony Hobson evidently sent copies of this article to a number of Yates

Thompson's relatives and we have their replies and comments at Sotheby's, including Yates Thompson's purchase prices for most of his books, supplied by his nephew Sir Christopher Chancellor. Thirdly there is the fine chapter 16, 'Manuscript Milestone', by my fellow speaker at this conference, Frank Herrmann, in his history of Sotheby's, 1980, to which I owe not least this description of Yates Thompson, taken from *The Times* obituary:

First impressions of the large head, short, compact build, square, broad shoulders, the direct glance, shrewd and penetrating under the heavy brows, the sudden glint of laughter lighting up the grim, bearded countenance, the gruff voice and the bluntness, almost rudeness, of address soon yielded to recognition of the breadth of his interests and the richness of his experience....

Frank Herrmann adds: 'Towards the end of his life Yates Thompson looked for all the world like a retired sea-dog with his full white beard, his unusually slit-like eyes, his highly polished boots, and his peppery temperament. He had a marvellous sense of humour, loved teasing his friends, and was quite happy to be nick-named "the Pound of Tea"'.[7] My great-grandfather knew him, and I think I would have liked to do so too.

Yates Thompson always claimed that his passion for antiquarian books came from his maternal grandfather Joseph Brooks Yates, of Liverpool, son of a unitarian minister and a very successful West Indies merchant, antiquarian, and philanthropist. Yates Thompson published a portrait of him in 1912, acknowledging that his 'example made me a collector of MSS'.[8] Old Yates died in December 1855, bequeathing ten illuminated manuscripts to his grandson, who received them in 1856, when he was only 18, a good age to begin bibliophily. They were: a 13th-century Bible; a very interesting if rough 13th-century English Missal from Lessness Abbey in Kent (now in the Victoria and Albert Museum); a Roman de la Rose, with 29 miniatures; two minor manuscripts from Santa Justina in Padua (one was given by Yates Thompson to Newnham College in Cambridge in 1902); a fine and unusual Venetian Cicero dated 1448-9 given by Yates Thompson to the Athenaeum in Liverpool in 1898; a Florentine Ovid of 1457, written for Lorenzo Ridolphi and afterwards owned by Chester Beatty and Eric Millar; a very curious Pseudo-Aristotle, Secreta Secretorum, illuminated in Genoa with 120 small historiated initials including one showing the artist himself, Fra Adam de Montaldo; and two spectacular Portolan atlases, one now in the Royal Geographical Society and the other in the Huntington in San Marino. Some of these manuscripts had been bought in London – at the Drury and Hanrott sales, for example – but one of the Portolans had been bought by Yates on a trip to Rome in 1826 and the other had been a present in 1850. These ten manuscripts were just the kind of books that a wealthy gentleman collector might own in the mid-19th century. They laid perhaps greater emphasis on curiosity than artistry. Grandfather Yates had published several antiquarian articles on manuscripts and emblem books, and the manuscripts in his own library were generally inexpensive but enhanced by mostly having original provenances and/or the names of their scribes.

The young Henry Yates Thompson added nothing to this inheritance until 1879. He had been working and travelling, as we have seen, but having married in 1878 began to settle down in Portman Square. In February of that year he bought a Book of Hours in Paris from the dealer Joseph Techener, his first Book of Hours (his grandfather had not had one), a good if not spectacular first purchase for a new collector: about 1470, Flemish for the Spanish market, with 24 Calendar scenes and 15 full-page miniatures. His next was also bought in Paris, seven years later, also a Book of Hours but a rather better one, Parisian, with miniatures by the Master of Jean Rolin II, and it belonged subsequently to Dyson Perrins and now to the Comites Latentes collection in Geneva. When Yates Thompson bought it he was 47 years old and it was now 30 years since his grandfather had died, and the Book of Hours was still perhaps not much more than a casual purchase on a spring outing to Paris. In October that year he bought a third Book of Hours, this time in London from Sotheran, c. 1460, made perhaps in Amiens in a Flemish binding signed by Jacobus de Gavere. In October two years later Yates Thompson was back in Paris and bought a second Pseudo-Aristotle, Secreta Secretorum (adding it to the copy from his grandfather's bequest), written and illuminated in Italian style with grisaille borders, then believed to be Italian but now recognised as one of those English proto-humanist books made in London by the Italian scribe Milo de Carraria in the late 1440s. It is in a contemporary decorated binding: 'said to be camel's hide', wrote Henry Yates Thompson,[9] probably for the first time caught up in the romance of medieval manuscripts.

A year and a half later again, early in 1893, he seems to have met Bernard Quaritch, the supreme salesman of medieval manuscripts for whom Yates Thompson represented the perfect material for developing into a serious collector. He sold him a 13th-century Bible in March, and M.R. James observed that its Litany pointed to Fécamp in Normandy. Then in December he sold him two more, a further Book of Hours and the great 14th-century Apocalypse which had belonged to the Duke of Sussex and has 70 oblong miniatures of great quality. Quaritch charged £250, not excessive. Yates Thompson returned on Friday 6 January and bought the Psalter of

Cosimo de'Medici. Quaritch had owned it since the Tite sale of 1874 and had evidently been unable to sell it, though it featured in three catalogues. Perhaps he told his new customer a different story for Yates Thompson later recalled 'This was a favourite book of the late Mr. Bernard Quaritch, and he parted with it to me in 1894 with genuine regret',[10] charging (incidentally) £260 probably with no regret at all. On the Monday Yates Thompson was back again. He bought for another £260 the mid-15th century Wingfield Hours – thus he spent not far off a thousand pounds with Quaritch in under three weeks – and evidently much enjoyed himself taking it round to G.F. Warner at the British Museum where they identified the original devices as those of Humphrey Stafford, first Duke of Buckingham. Yates Thompson himself, rising to the first of his many antiquarian forays into his own collection, traced through the family descent to the Richard Wingfield for whom it had been bound in the 16th century.[11] In April Yates Thompson bought another Book of Hours, the Dunois Hours, from Ellis & Elvey who had just issued a privately-printed little book about it, recounting its romantic origin with Jean, comte de Dunois, the Bastard of Orléans, son of the Duke of Orléans assassinated in 1407, and of Mariette, wife of Sir Aubert de Cany. The provenance is a remarkable one, and the 91 large and small miniatures are first-class. Francis Wormald called it 'certainly one of the finest French manuscripts in existence.'[12] Ellis followed this up quickly by selling Yates Thompson a fine Cicero illuminated for Piero di Lorenzo de'Medici, another magnificent provenance carried home to Portman Square.

By now, 1894, Yates Thompson was evidently completely hooked on illuminated manuscripts and he began to spend increasingly large sums on books with high quality illumination or romantic or aristocratic first owners. I have compiled for my own amusement a list of his purchases arranged in order of acquisition. There are ten manuscripts bought in 1894, 17 in 1895, and ten more in 1896. Some of these were purchased abroad, like the Hours of Nicholas von Firmian which he bought in Naples in the summer of 1894 for the then huge sum of £500 (it was re-sold at Sotheby's in 1980 for £48,000), and the Poupaincourt Hours which he bought in December 1896 in San Remo (and which came back in the Dyson Perrins sale in 1959 for £4,800). He bought one item in the Spitzer sale in Paris in 1895, the Tilliot Hours of about 1530 with 56 large and small miniatures by or intimately associated with the artist Jean Poyet of Tours. Janet Backhouse, who has published three accounts of this manuscript, comments on how unfashionable was French renaissance art in the 1890s and how perceptive was Yates Thompson's choice.[13] Other manuscripts were dispatched to Yates Thompson from the dealers Morgand and Belin and Techener, all in Paris. But by far the largest number were now acquired in London from Bernard Quaritch – including for £100 the Lusher Psalter, which had been on Quaritch's shelves for 15 years, for £400 the outstanding twelfth-century Ottobeuren Collectarius which Quaritch had been unable to sell for six years, the Brégilles Hours which had been for sale since 1886, for £190 the Cassiodorus of Leo X which Quaritch had owned for nine years, for £375 the Bentivoglio Bible which had been in Quaritch's stock since 1880, and so on and on, often several a month, enriching his own collection with some of the finest illuminated manuscripts and doubtless causing much delight and relief to Mr Quaritch and his bank manager.

In two bites, in the autumn of 1895 and the summer of 1896, Yates Thompson bought privately in Paris (I get the impression it was through the agency of Gustave Pawlowski) seven unsold lots from the supreme collection of the late publisher Firmin Didot whose library had been dispersed at auction between 1877 and 1881. The bought-in lots – the b.i.'s as they were (and still are) called in the trade – had been retained by the Didot family. Yates Thompson paid £280 for the Hours of Anthony of Burgundy (b.i. in 1879 for 7,000 francs), £540 for the 14th-century Sainte-Abbaye (b.i. in the same sale for 13,100 francs), £320 for the Hours of René II of Lorraine (b.i. for 6,000 francs), £150 for a 13th-century crusader chronicle of William of Tyre with 25 miniatures and a second later copy with 49 miniatures; and he acquired thus a splendid quarto French Boethius (now in the Gulbenkian Foundation), and a very unusual Burgundian chronicle with 11 miniatures, perhaps from the Burgundian ducal library, which had originally been found walled up in a cupboard of a house in Dijon in the mid-19th century. It is now in the British Library.

This *en bloc* haul of Firmin Didot manuscripts in 1895-6 may have inspired Yates Thompson into his single most extraordinary *coup* which took place in May 1897 when he acquired the entire residue of some 210 manuscripts from the equally great and celebrated library of Lord Ashburnham. I must not lose the thread of my tale by getting too entangled in following back the Ashburnham collection, but, whatever the title of my paper, one can state that without qualification the great bibliophile fourth Earl of Ashburnham, who died in 1878, was an absolute gentleman. His life has been magisterially recounted by the late Dr A.N.L. Munby who conjures the image of the autocratic, upright, aloof, proud, disdainful nobleman, who regarded Sir Thomas Phillipps and the Bishop of Chichester and his Master of the Foxhounds as equally beneath contempt.[14] Ashburnham acquired several entire libraries of manuscripts – from Libri, Barrois and Stowe, respectively (all these are part of another story) – but his own collection of manuscripts, bought one by one, he called the *Appendix* and he issued a privately-printed morocco-bound handlist of them in 1861. There were about 210 manuscripts there in 1897. The most remarkable, the late 9th-century Lindau Gospels, was sold for £10,000 to Pierpont Morgan, his manuscript 1, and the remaining 209 volumes (approximately: it is difficult to be exactly sure) were sold for £30,000 to Henry Yates Thompson. It is hard to convey the magnitude of this purchase in the 1890s. £30,000 was the equivalent of a truly multi-million pound deal, and really these were multi-millionaires' manuscripts.

There were two results of the purchase. The first was that Yates Thompson could now enjoy a selection of the finest conceivable manuscripts in the best possible condition – the absolute pickings of the wealthiest bibliophile in England half a century before. Yates Thompson could thus share Ashburnham's snobbery and need concentrate only on the very very best. The second result was that he now had too many manuscripts, and the collection was unmanageable. By my counting he had acquired 59 manuscripts up until the Ashburnham purchase. In the summer of 1897 he suddenly had a quarter of a thousand manuscripts.

Yates Thompson therefore evolved what has become the most famous feature of his collection, the total of a Hundred Manuscripts. He would restrict the collection to exactly one hundred volumes, all of the best possible quality, and would dispose of everything else. He would, however, continue to collect, and as finer pieces were acquired at the upper end of the range, so the lesser items at the bottom of the Hundred would be sold off and the collection would be constantly upgrading itself while always retaining exactly one hundred items. This explains all those sales at the beginning of this paper between 1899 – when he relieved himself of no less than 177 Ashburnham manuscripts – and 1914, when the outbreak of war put a temporary stop to this eternal buying and weeding.

What is unusual (maybe even disconcerting in defining a gentleman collector) is the way that Yates Thompson seems always to have known and recorded the exact prices he paid for his books and the profits when he sold them. A gentleman never discusses money or religion, one used to be told. In every manuscript Yates Thompson recorded in ink his price in simple code (the code word was BRYANSTONE). He was a rich, but not a supremely rich man. Nowadays one cannot collect seriously without being aware of the cost and recouping some of the expense when appropriate. The practice of Yates Thompson is very common now but was strange in the gentlemanly circles of Edwardian bibliophily. Probably Yates Thompson marks the moment when illuminated manuscripts became so expensive that a dilettante gentleman could no longer afford to collect them. Yates Thompson recollected in old age that he had 'expended in this collection a sum of money decidedly larger than I had any business to spend on a private whim'.[15] The succession of weeding sales were probably quite necessary for the comfort of the Yates Thompson household.

The 35 or so manuscripts which Yates Thompson kept from the Ashburnham Appendix included the Carrow Psalter of about 1240, the Spanish Beatus on the Apocalypse dated 894, the 14th-century Taymouth Hours, the Hours of Elizabeth the Quene, the Duc de Berry's *Bible Historiale*, the Duc de Berry's Vincent of Beauvais (which in our lifetimes H.P. Kraus swapped for the two Fust and Schoeffer Psalters in the Bibliothèque Nationale), and the astonishing Hours of Queen Joan of Navarre, *c.*1340, with 108 miniatures, which Edmond de Rothschild bought in the 1919 sale for £11,800, by far the highest price then ever paid for any illuminated manuscript and the holder of the record for many years.

As he constantly sorted his collection, adding items to the Hundred and ruthlessly discarding others, so one can see Yates Thompson's judgement in action. Out went all but two of his grandfather's manuscripts, even the Roman de la Rose having been superseded by the Ashburnham copy. On the other hand, he kept his Didot Boethius, discarding the richer but not as well painted Ashburnham volume. Nothing bought before 1891 was retained. In came four manuscripts from William Morris's sale in 1898, and two were later discarded again. In came his great Dante bought in May 1901, written for King Alfonso of Aragon with 85 miniatures by Giovanni di Paolo. In came five books bought from Ruskin's estate in 1902 including the Beaupré Antiphoner for £1,200 and the Hours of Isabella of France for £2,000. He was intrigued by books associated with women, and kept a copy of Christine de Pisan, although (he explained) 'the volume is scarcely up to the level of my collection, and I should not have bought it had it not been for my desire to possess a copy of one of Christine's works';[16] and he used to suggest that his Hours of Joan of Navarre might have been painted by the royal painter Bourgot *enlumineuresse*, daughter of Jean le Noir. Anything with a royal or princely provenance was retained by Yates Thompson. He had three books which once belonged to the Duc de Berry, and others from the libraries of Yolande of Flanders; Charles V; Humfrey Duke of Gloucester; Prigent de Coetivy, Admiral of France; Louis of Anjou; Anthony of Burgundy; Pius II; Cosimo de'Medici; Ercole d'Este, Duke of Ferrara; and Dionora, Duchess of Urbino. He retained the Hours of Anthony of Burgundy, illegitimate son of Philip the Good, simply for that reason although its miniatures, as M.R. James said, were 'not of marked excellence'.[17] He kept a second-rate Psalter because the royal arms on the binding seemed to indicate that it had belonged to Henry VIII, the arms being, he explained, 'I suspect, what got it into my Hundred manuscripts'.[18] He admired the gem-like Credo of Charles V (as it was called on remarkably slight evidence) 'for its association with a great name'.[19] The whole of the fifth volume of Yates Thompson's *Illustration* in 1915 comprised manuscripts which had 'belonged to some Individual of Note' in France or Italy in the Middle Ages, dukes and princes and popes. It might be that, if one were to be as much of a snob as Lord Ashburnham, that this purchasing of kinship with the aristocrats of the past is like the Victorian not-quite-gentlemen who bought and luxuriated in their family trees. When he did not know the medieval owner of one of his books, Yates Thompson judged by the quality of the book that the possessor was quite obviously, as he put it, 'a gentleman of taste'.[20] I am sure that Yates Thompson saw himself as that.

There is every evidence that Yates Thompson knew his manuscripts extremely well. He recognised Coetivy and Armagnac provenances overlooked by the booksellers. He poked around the bishop's palace in Ceneda on the edge of Venice in 1901 noting that the bishop's arms differed from those in his Calderini Pontifical, bought in 1898. He quite rightly recognised the hand of Jean Fouquet in an *Histoire Ancienne* fragment from the Crawford of Lakelands collection in 1903. He gave the Sandars Lectures in Cambridge in 1901 and 1904. He had a very good visual memory and delighted in recognising and matching up different and separated portions from the same manuscripts, claiming to have 'met with some half-dozen cases in forming my own collection';[21] thus, for example, reuniting the two parts of the Armagnac Breviary separated before 1848, and noting missing portions of his own books in Lyons Cathedral, the British Museum, the Bibliothèque Nationale, and elsewhere. A great story of matching manuscripts concerns the second volume of an illustrated Josephus which he bought at Sotheby's in March 1903. The Sotheby's cataloguer had failed to recognise even that the volume had belonged to the Duc de Berry and the book fell to Yates Thompson, bidding through Cockerell, for £50. Then begins the fun. The book had descended to Jacques d'Armagnac (Yates Thompson recognised this) who had further miniatures added around 1475. Volume I proved to be in the Bibliothèque Nationale, ms.fr.247, one of the most famous of all French 15th-century books because it has the supremely important contemporary inscription saying the later miniatures were supplied by Jean Fouquet, painter to Louis XI and native of Tours, the sole documentary evidence for the hand of the greatest French medieval artist. The one remaining miniature in Yates Thompson's half is in the same hand

and thus by Fouquet too. But Yates Thompson collated his book and noted that 12 miniatures were missing and that they must have been removed while the book was in England, and in 1904 he wrote and afterwards printed an extraordinary challenge: 'I would willingly give and hereby offer' (he said) 'the same sum that I gave for the volume (viz: – £50) to anybody who shall tell me where they are. In this age of Booksellers, Librarians, Amateurs and Catalogues, it ought not to be difficult to discover them, provided always that they exist'.[22] It worked. In 1905 George Warner found ten of the missing twelve Fouquet miniatures at Windsor Castle in an album which had been presented to Queen Victoria. There was no chance of buying them and so instead Yates Thompson gave his volume to the King on the condition that the miniatures be reinserted and the composite book be presented by Edward VII to the President of France, which it was in Paris in March 1906, and thus Yates Thompson's half was rejoined with Volume I in the Bibliothèque Nationale, now ms.nouv.acq.fr.21013. For this act, Yates Thompson became a *chevalier* of the *légion d'honneur*, and therefore also became a gentleman of France. (I should add as a footnote that two miniatures of the twelve are still missing, and are most likely in England, and if you should recognise them in an antique shop somewhere – which any of you might – you would get £300,000 to £500,000 each for them, I think; or you might prefer the *légion d'honneur* from M. Mitterand.)

Once he had decided on his Hundred Manuscripts, Yates Thompson began to publish at his own expense from Cambridge University Press, a series of catalogues of his manuscripts with scholarly (if slightly dull) descriptions mostly by M.R. James (who was paid 5 guineas a manuscript he described) and by Sydney Cockerell, with help where appropriate from W.H.J. Weale, Edmund Maunde Thompson, Yates Thompson himself, and others, the first volume in 1898, the second in 1902, the third in 1907, and the last in 1912.[23] These are difficult to use because by the time the next volume was out, many of the items in the previous volume had been sold to make room within the Hundred for new acquisitions. Yates Thompson also published not only a Roxburghe Club book but also individual studies of specific manuscripts printed at the Chiswick Press, and surviving mostly in inscribed presentation copies. In 1907 he began to issue a new series of eight slim folios, *Illustrations of One Hundred Manuscripts in the Library of Henry Yates Thompson*, the first volume in 100 numbered copies, the second in 125, and the third to eighth, which was issued in 1918, without limitation.[24] They are handsome books but when you open them widely the pages tend to snap off and drop out. All these catalogues made Yates Thompson's collection without question the best-known private collection in the world.

If, as a cynic might suggest, Yates Thompson was not entirely a gentleman in his bibliophily but had an eye to weeding and re-selling, this publicity was entirely in his favour. This idea of publishing illustrated scholarly catalogues of a private collection was I think entirely new then, but the success was followed by Dyson Perrins in 1920, Chester Beatty in 1927-30, Major Abbey in 1969, and Peter Ludwig in 1979-85, and in every case the eventual sale results were incidentally greatly enhanced by the fame of the various collections.

The last Yates Thompson catalogue included a separate postscript with the then astonishing announcement that the collector now intended to sell his entire collection by auction. The reaction from the scholarly world was one of outrage, and is chronicled in some detail both by Josiah Bennett and by Frank Herrmann and so I shall not elaborate here except in so far as it is relevant to the theme of 'Was Yates Thompson a Gentleman?' Cockerell vigorously rushed in to disapprove, saying that intact the collection was 'one of the great artistic and spiritual assets of England', and M.R. James urged Yates Thompson to think again, writing 'I did think they were at least safe for England and were not, once gathered, to be dispersed again among the Boches, Jews and Transatlantics'.[25] The implication is interesting: that a gentleman is patriotic, 'in England' (as de Ricci wrote as late as 1930) 'to be a collector has nearly always meant – to be a patriot',[26] and that to be unpatriotic was ungentlemanly, and that to let manuscripts fall into the hands of Germans or Jews or Americans was to allow them to pass into the hands of people who were frankly not gentlemanly. That Yates Thompson should own manuscripts privately was commendable, but to risk common people buying them was unforgivable. It is extraordinary what a change of attitude has come about in the last 70 years.

As an auctioneer I cannot enter into this debate except to record that the three Yates Thompson sales brought record prices over and over again. The first sale in 1919 made £52,360 in an hour and a half. The next sale in 1920 made £75,265. The third sale in 1921 added another £18,024. Josiah Bennett implies that Yates Thompson's motive in selling was commercial, but *The Daily Telegraph* and certainly the relatives to whom Anthony Hobson sent Mr Bennett's article all agreed that Yates Thompson decided to part with his books because failing eyesight had robbed him of the pleasure of enjoying them (he was now over 80), and the *Telegraph* piece went on that Yates Thompson 'wished to enjoy the thrill of hearing the progressive bidding in the auction room testifying the approval of the world's collectors; yet he sat like a sphinx'.[27] His great-niece recollected in 1967 that as a young girl she had been sent to the first sale as a guide to her half-blind uncle because his wife could not bear to go herself. Once again, it was very unusual in 1919 (even perhaps not quite the thing to do) for a collector to arrange his own sale, rather than waiting until he was dead, like a gentleman. Since then it has become commonplace: Chester Beatty, Abbey, Boise Penrose, Honeyman, and even Cockerell all sent their manuscripts to Sotheby's in their lifetime. Having witnessed his own sale, Yates Thompson passed the final ten years of his old age in tranquillity. The unsold lots from the auction and the residue of Yates Thompson's manuscripts were bequeathed by his widow to the British Museum in 1941 on the condition that they be displayed and catalogued. I am sure they are appreciated, but there is still no catalogue of them and when I looked last Thursday not one Yates Thompson manuscript was on exhibition.

In conclusion, was Yates Thompson a gentleman? The answer is yes of course, in modern terms absolutely and unequivocally the quintessential Victorian and Edwardian gentleman, but in his time maybe an unusual collector with commercial motives just a shade larger than was common then. Constant buying and selling have to be part of the process of manuscript collecting in the 20th century, and in that sense Yates Thompson was the first modern bibliophile. Of his taste there is no doubt; he was probably the most refined English manuscript collector ever, and the quality of his Hundred Manuscripts secures his absolute immortality.

References

1. 1 May 1899, Ashburnham Appendix sale, lots 1-177; 11 May 1901, lots 1-19; 14 May 1902, lots 1-42; 30 March 1903, lots 1-48; 3 May 1904, lots 1-56; 1 June 1905, lots 654-697; 17 December 1908, lots 289-296; 28 March 1912, lots 451-457; 25 June 1914, lots 1-2; 3 June 1919, lots 1-30; 24 March 1920, lots 31-64; 22 June 1921, lots 65-95. There was a posthumous sale of miscellaneous printed books and a few manuscripts on 18-19 August 1941, lots 1-526.
2. J.Q. Bennett, 'Portman Square to New Bond Street, or, How to Make Money though Rich', The Book Collector, XVI, 1967, p.328.
3. Ibid, p.324.
4. Dictionary of National Biography, Twentieth Century, 1922-1930, Oxford, 1937, pp.836-7. Nigel Ramsey kindly tells me of a eulogy of Mrs Yates Thompson by Elizabeth Robins, Portrait of a Lady, or The English Spirit Old and New, London, 1941. I am grateful to Charles Sebag-Montefiore for drawing my attention to Yates Thompson's privately printed An Illustrated Catalogue of Pictures and Portraits now at 19 Portman Square, London, 1921, which includes a view of the library in Portman Square with bookcases to the left of the fireplace with tantalising glimpses of neat polished rows of ancient leather spines (Pl.1.)
5. Les manuscrits de la collection Henry Yates Thompson, Paris, 1926.

6. Cited above, notes 2-3; full page reference is pp.323-39.

7. F. Herrmann, *Sotheby's, Portrait of an Auction House*, London, 1980, p.185.

8. *A Descriptive Catalogue of Fourteen Illuminated Manuscripts, nos.XCV to CVII and 79A, Completing the Hundred in the Library of Henry Yates Thompson*, Cambridge, 1912. frontispiece; the same portrait is propped up on the mantlepiece in the view of Yates Thompson's library in 1921, cited above, note 4.

9. *Illustrations from One Hundred Manuscripts*, II, London, 1908, p.15; it is now Fitzwilliam Museum MS.42-1950.

10. Yates Thompson in footnote to Sotheby's, 23 March 1920, p.131, lot 62; the manuscript is now Fitzwilliam Museum MS.3-1950.

11. It is now New York Public Library Spenser MS.3.

12. F. Wormald, 'The Yates Thompson Manuscripts', *British Museum Quarterly*, XVI, 1951, p.5; the manuscript is now B.L. Yates Thompson MS 3.

13. J. Backhouse, 'The Tilliot Hours: Comparisons and Relationships', *British Library Journal*, XIII, 1987, p.229, the full reference being pp.211-31; and cf. her articles on the same manuscript, now B.L. Yates Thompson MS 5, in J. Trapp (ed.), *Manuscripts in the Fifty Years after the Invention of Printing*, London, 1983, pp.175-80, and in T. Kren (ed.), *Renaissance Painting in Manuscripts*, New York, 1983, pp.175-80.

14. 'The Earl and the Thief', in N. Barker (ed.), A.N.L. Munby, *Essays and Papers*, London, 1978, pp.175-91.

15. Writing to M.R. James; cited by Bennett, p.326, and by Herrmann, p.188.

16. H.Y. Thompson, *A Descriptive Catalogue of Twenty Illuminated Manuscripts, nos.LXXV to XCIV*, Cambridge, 1907, p.35.

17. M.R. James, *A Descriptive Catalogue of Fifty Manuscripts from the Collection of Henry Yates Thompson*, Cambridge, 1898, p.59.

18. *Illustrations from One Hundred Manuscripts... The Seventh and Last Volume*, London, 1918, p.5. W.H.J. Weale had observed that the portion dating from Henry VIII's reign was of 'inferior execution'. The manuscript itself is now B.L. Yates Thompson MS 18.

19. Sotheby's, 22 June 1921, p.204, footnote to lot 94; the manuscript was re-sold at Sotheby's in Monaco, 5 December 1987, lot 232.

20. *Illustrations... Seventh and Last Volume*, London, 1918, p.5, describing the Psalter and Hours now B.L. Yates Thompson MS 15.

21. *Ibid*, p.6.

22. Cited by Yates Thompson, *A Descriptive Catalogue of Twenty Illuminated Manuscripts, nos.LXXV to XCIV*, Cambridge, 1907, p.6.

23. Cited above in notes 8, 16, 17 and 22.

24. Cited above in notes 9, 18 and 20.

25. Bennett, p.325; Herrmann, p.187.

26. S. de Ricci, *English Collectors of Books and Manuscripts (1530-1930) and their Marks of Ownership*, Cambridge, 1930, p.193.

27. Herrmann, p.190.

T. Bardwell pinx.   *P. Audinet sculp*

Tho: Martin

of Palgrave   *Born 1696 ? died 1771*

'If Lavater's system of physiognomy happen to receive your approbation, you will conclude, upon contemplating Tom's frank countenance ... that the collector of Palgrave must have been a "fine old fellow".' T.F. Dibdin, *Bibliomania*.

The ill-gotten library of 'Honest Tom' Martin

DAVID STOKER

THE NAME of Thomas Martin is occasionally to be found in accounts of English book collectors of the 18th century, although often only as a footnote or passing reference.[1] Such references usually note his unusual sobriquet, 'Honest Tom', and record that for 40 years he had custody of the valuable Le Neve collection of manuscripts. Comparatively little has been written about Martin's own collecting activities, or the extent to which he added to the Le Neve collection. It is not generally realised that for a decade from the early 1750s he possessed one of the three or four most valuable private libraries in England. Yet by the early 1760s he had to sell off parts of his library. Within a few years of his death in 1771 the remaining books and manuscripts had been so totally dispersed as to make it difficult now to have any conception of its richness. This paper will therefore consider Tom Martin and his library: its acquisition, administration, the uses to which it was put, and the fate that befell it. However, it is first necessary to describe the man himself, for he was far from being a typical antiquarian and book collector.

Tom Martin was a skilled and intelligent attorney who hated practising law. He rather devoted all his energies, together with several small fortunes, to his two passions – strong drink, and the collecting of historical antiquities. He came from the part of Thetford lying in the county of Suffolk.[2] He was born 8 March 1696/7, the son of a well to do clergyman.[3] As a young man he hoped to go to Cambridge, where his family had connections with Caius College.[4] However, his father chose a career for him in his elder brother's legal practice in the town. About 1722 he married a wealthy young widow. The following year they moved to the Suffolk village of Palgrave (close to the Norfolk market town of Diss), where he remained until his death in 1771.

Two quotations from the antiquary William Cole, will serve to describe his character.

He is a blunt, rough, honest downright man; of no behaviour or guile: often drunk in a morning with strong beer, and for breakfast, when others had tea or coffee, he had beef steaks, or other strong meat. – His thirst after antiquities was as great as after liquors: the one injured his fortune, as the other did health.[5]

Similarly:

Mr Martin has an house at Thetford also at Palgrave. I once spent a week with him. An attorney of good practice, & would be better, was he not too much given to drinking. However he is an honest man, & of a curious inquisitive turn in all matters relating to antiquity, which has rather injured his fortune as it is supposed. For tho' he had a good private fortune of his own, independent of his practice, which he made away with & was again set up by a very good estate which fell to him, yet such was his thirst after curiosities in the antiquary way, that it is supposed he has hurt himself again.[6]

Martin displayed many of the symptoms of an alcoholic, for according to Sir John Fenn,

When he began what he called a frolic, he would never give up whilst his money lasted, but would continue it for days and nights together, treating and carousing with porters, chairmen and persons of the lowest rank, to whom you might often find him (when surrounded in the porter cellar) telling stories and singing songs with every degree of humour suited to his company.

After an adventure of this kind he would *latterly* lie in bed for a considerable time, lament his imprudence, eat little, and drink only water.[7]

Martin's constitution must have been quite robust in spite of the damage he is supposed to have done to his health. At the age of 65 he still had

so great a pliancy of limbs that he could turn his foot so as to place a glass of liquor on the sole of it and drink it off.[8]

At the same time it could also be said of him that:

As an antiquary, he was most skilful and indefatigable; and when he was employed as an attorney and genealogist, he was in his element.... He had the happiest use of his pen, copying, as well as tracing, with dispatch and exactness, the different writing of every aera, and tricking arms, seals, &c, with great neatness. His taste for antient lore seems to have possessed him from his earliest to his latest days. He dated all the scraps of paper on which he made his church notes, & c. Some of these begin as early as 1721, and end but the autumn before his death, when he still wrote an excellent hand; but he certainly began his collections even before the first mentioned period,...[9]

Among his papers are large numbers of facsimiles of charters, together with other documents, and drawings of coins or seals.[10]

Nearly all the surviving biographical accounts of Martin, and references to him in the correspondence of the leading antiquaries and historians of his day, remark upon his two apparently insatiable appetites. Curiously, they also frequently allude to his 'honesty'. In 1737, the historian Francis Blomefield wrote to explain his non-appearance at a friend's house thus:

At the time I design'd I set out with Honest Tom Martin in order for Darsingham but the weather proving bad & having the good fortune to load ourselves with antiquity before we reached Lynn, and my companion losing 2 days there by loading himself with a stronger tho' not heavier burthen. I determined to return, & wait on you in the spring.[11]

This then was 'Honest' Tom Martin,[12] a 'Squire Western' figure of the antiquarian world, who was yet renowned among the great historians of his time; a cherished member of the Society of Antiquaries for 53 years.[13]

Although other examples of Martin's 'frolics' are recorded by Fenn and Cullum, less detail is given about his literary pursuits, and in particular, his magpie-like obsession with collecting historical materials. These included not only printed and manuscript books, but documents of all kinds, prints, paintings, or any artefact with historical associations which his wife would allow in the house. His collection of coins and tokens was so renowned that Francis Blomefield used it as an additional attraction when writing to invite his numismatist friends to visit him.[14] The sale of his property also included such varied items as an Indian tomahawk, various medieval weapons, Roman urns, lamps, spurs, horse bits, pieces of sculpture, a sword-fish, sea shells, fossils, petrifactions, and an ostrich egg.[15]

It was an undirected fascination providing him with an enormous working knowledge of English antiquities and a reference library which was the envy of many contemporary historians. Yet at the same time it disabled him from any limited field of study. He never published anything in his lifetime, in spite of often claiming to 'have several things upon the anvil which I have hopes of publishing'.[16] In 1743 he boasted to John Tanner,

As for my part (was it not for my family) I could be content to live almost on bread and water the remainder of my days, so I might have leisure to publish only some Fragmenta Antiquitatis, which I have amassed together, and an Appendix to Mr. Blomefield's History of Thetford, &c.[17]

However, the history of Thetford bearing his name was compiled on his behalf from the many notes he had collected on the subject but had never managed to write up.[18]

Even in his historical collecting, the rough and ready character of the man comes through, as is shown by the following excerpt from one of thousands of loose sheets that he added to his library, each containing pieces of information he considered worthy of record.

On Tuesday Morning [24th September 1751] came to
the Crown in Swaffham

Wall the Spanish Embassador	Lord Anson
His Grace the Duke of Grafton	Jeffries Esqr
Lord Euston his Grandson	Southcoate Esqr
Lord De La Ware	Furneis Esqr
Lord Leicester	

They came from Euston Hall and were going to Lord
Leicesters at Holkham.
Lord Delaware had a wooden nose on such as the Buffoons use, which he put on and took off at pleasure. His Grace of G----n was observ'd to make water twice the short time they staid at Swaffham (to drink a dish of coffee, and change horses &c) in doing which office (the second time, under his chariot), several spectators (inter quo ipse sui) observ'd his p---- (for the size whereof he has been remarkably famous). It was short, but surprisingly thick, of a swarthy complexion, and look'd something like the end of a collar'd eel, before 'tis cut asunder.[19]

Background

Martin appears to have been a born antiquary, collector, and librarian. He was largely self taught, having had a sorely neglected education. For many years he was the only pupil at the Thetford free school, being left to read on his own.[20] Among his papers, there survives a notebook written in a youthful hand entitled 'A catalogue of mine and my father's books which I use' later annotated 'written when a school boy'. It contains 84 titles.[21] Otherwise his leisure time seems to have been spent in exploring the many ruins and other relics of the past in the town. As he commented in a letter lamenting his lot, 'I'm sure there can be no worse town under the sun for breeding and conversation'.[22]

About 1710 Thetford was visited by the elderly Peter Le Neve, Norroy King of Arms, first President of the revived Society of Antiquaries. He sought a guide to the many antiquities of the town only to be told that no-one knew more than 13-year-old Master Martin.[23] The result was the growth of a close friendship between the learned old man and the teenage boy lasting until the death of the former. This served also to encourage the antiquarian leanings of the latter.

As a young man Martin soon became an avid purchaser of books and manuscripts for his private library. Many lists of such purchases made by Martin from London or provincial booksellers, book auctions, and private collectors dating from 1720 onwards survive in the Norfolk Record Office.[24] However, his serious collecting seems to have coincided with his astute marriage and move to Palgrave two years later. The Suffolk Record Office holds a detailed personal account book by him for the period from 1726 to 1731, indicating in great detail how he spent every penny of his money.[25]

He also became interested in, and adept at, the organisation and classification of large documentary collections. At different times in his life he reorganised several, including his own. In fact the only lengthy period he spent away from his native Suffolk appears to have been during the Summer and Autumn of 1724 when he was paid 30 pounds by the authorities of Eton College for setting the muniment room in order and compiling a digest of many of the records there. The staff at Eton still value his work which is recorded by a wooden plaque in the library.[26]

Martin's Library

At its height, around 1761, Martin's private library probably consisted of about 12,000 printed books and several thousand manuscript volumes. In addition it included many tens (perhaps hundreds) of thousands of unbound documents. During the intervening period he had brought up two large families, (he married twice within a decade, each of his wives bearing him eight children, about half of whom lived to adulthood). As a well-to-do young lawyer, with such family responsibilities, he might have built up a respectable library, but he would never have been able to amass a collection on this scale by legal means. The true origin of much of Martin's library lay not with the attorney himself, but rather with his rich elderly friend, Peter Le Neve. The irregular way in which Le Neve's manuscripts came into Martin's possession (the circumstances of which were perhaps known to at least some of Martin's circle) makes his nickname seem something of a joke.

Peter Le Neve had intended to write the topographical history of Norfolk and had devoted the greater part of his life to collecting materials for the task. He spent years systematically searching for, and indexing, Norfolk references in the major series of Public Records. In addition, as Norroy King of Arms he also had access to the genealogical and heraldic manuscripts of the College of Arms. However, in spite of his enormous scholarship and capacity for study, he also, like his young friend Thomas

Martin, had a temperament unsuited to writing an historical narrative. Le Neve published nothing during his lifetime. His obsessional gathering of as much material as possible meant that at the time of his death in 1729 he had built up an enormous collection of manuscripts. Richard Gough later described it as 'the greatest fund of antiquities for his native county that ever was collected for any single one in the kingdom'.[27] It was this accumulation which fell into Martin's hands.

Le Neve's Norfolk (and to a lesser extent Suffolk) collections fell into three broad categories.[28] He had many original historical documents such as cartularies, feodaries and manorial court rolls. Secondly, he had created a series of calendars and indexes to Norfolk and Suffolk references in the Public Records, and College of Arms. Finally, there was a truly massive jumble of miscellaneous information on tiny slips or scraps of paper, compiled from a vast array of sources by many different hands, and thousands of other loose papers. These were all organised in a crude topographical order.

Many of these slips had been written by Le Neve or his amanuensis, or one of the circle of 'Icenian' antiquaries with whom he corresponded and regularly exchanged notes. (This group included men such as John Kirkpatrick, Benjamin Mackerell, Thomas Tanner and Thomas Martin).[29] Many, however, consisted of the dissected notes of earlier antiquaries and similarly mutilated documents such as letters and accounts. Thus several historical collections by others (acquired by Le Neve during his lifetime) had been cut up for this crude filing system, making their origins impossible to trace.

Le Neve was a rich, but a cantankerous and eccentric man who whilst in his seventies had married a young and strong-willed wife. He frequently changed his mind about his will, particularly concerning his extensive library of printed books and manuscripts. At one time he intended to leave it all to the College of Arms, but later he changed his mind. As a result he left an imperfect will, which caused a long and expensive legal contest over the subsequent ownership of his estates. However, indisputably Le Neve intended his manuscripts relating to Norfolk and Suffolk to be available for public use. They were to be deposited within a year of his death in a suitable repository either in Norwich Cathedral or some other public building in the city.[30] To that end he appointed as Executors for this task his friends Thomas Tanner the Chancellor of the Diocese, and Thomas Martin. The will indicated that instructions for the disposal of the remainder of his literary and historical materials would be found in a note to be left in his writing desk prior to his decease.

The various Le Neve collections were, however, so extensive and ill-defined that Tom Martin, Thomas Tanner, and the young wife Prudence Le Neve, could not agree exactly what was included in each collection. They shelved the problem, pending the disposal of the printed books. Le Neve's note indicated that they were to be left to a distant relative in London, who promptly arranged to sell them by auction during the winter of 1730/1. Martin was one of the principal purchasers at this sale.[31]

Before and after the auction, Tom Martin was in his element. He spent many hours at his late friend's house in Great Witchingham, listing, examining and sorting the various manuscript collections, in much the same way as he had done at Eton College. However, by the autumn of 1731 (two years after Le Neve's death) the executors had still taken no action regarding the Norfolk and Suffolk manuscripts. Within a few months, however, this situation changed radically. In November Thomas Martin's first wife, Sarah, died soon after giving birth to twins, leaving him the care of eight young children. In December, Tanner heard he had been elevated to the see of St Asaph. He had quickly to wind up his affairs in Norfolk prior to his consecration at Lambeth on 23 January 1732: thereafter he never had the opportunity to return to his adopted county. In the same month of January the marriage of Thomas Martin and Prudence Le Neve not only solved the domestic problems of the former but had the added virtue of temporarily resolving the custody of the Norfolk and Suffolk manuscripts.[32]

After a short period the couple moved to Martin's house at Palgrave, taking with them the enormous manuscript collections destined for public use in Norwich, ostensibly until the question of their future custody could be resolved. Bishop Tanner was far from happy about the irregular way in which Martin and his wife had taken the manuscripts to Palgrave. However he could not do anything, unless he was willing to risk the cost of a Chancery suit against his co-executor, for the sake of a Diocese he had now left. In any event, other more valuable parts of Le Neve's considerable estate were already the subject of a costly lawsuit which eventually went to the House of Lords.

More than once Tanner wrote to Martin requesting that they should meet in London to discuss the matter.[33] Martin implied he would soon talk his wife into accepting Tanner's interpretation of the will.[34] However, partly as a result of the bishop's subsequent ill-health, Martin succeeded in delaying and ultimately avoiding any such meeting. Tanner's conscience was eased a little after 1733. He discovered that Martin was making the materials freely available to Francis Blomefield who had advertised the first of three topographical histories of East Anglian counties based upon them.[35]

However, Tanner was never completely reconciled to the situation up to his death in 1735. One side-effect of Martin's conduct was that the Bishop subsequently left all his manuscripts to the Bodleian Library rather than to Norwich Cathedral, much to the dismay of the Norfolk antiquarian community.[36]

In the introduction to the first volume of his history, Blomefield gratefully acknowledged Martin's help, both in providing material from his own collections, and also making available to him those of Le Neve, 'they resting in his hands until they be properly disposed of according to Mr. Le Neve's will'.[37] However, with no individual having any claim on the ownership, they were gradually amalgamated into Martin's own library and all thought of their being housed in a public repository was soon forgotten. This had clearly been Martin's intention, and indeed, within three years of their move to Palgrave, Blomefield was helping him dispose of a few choice items to private collectors.[38] It is not possible to say whether or not the nature of Martin's conduct was widely known among his contemporaries, although clearly at least some of the men who referred to him as 'Honest Tom' were aware of his malversation.

Further acquisitions

However, at the same time, and throughout the next 25 to 30 years, Martin was constantly adding to his collection by purchase and other means, for, as he said in a letter to Andrew Ducarel of December 1757, 'My numerous family and small income oblige me to be as frugal as possible; but wholly to abridge myself from buying some few books in the study I so much delight in, would be worse than imprisonment, or death itself.'[39] One might, however, question whether the amassing of more than 10,000 printed books over a 40 year period can fairly be described as 'buying some few books'.

Most of Martin's additions were of printed books, and in all learned subjects, although the emphasis was on British history. The sale catalogue of his printed books does, however, also contain substantial numbers of books in French, Spanish, Italian, Latin, Greek, Saxon, Arabic and Hebrew.[40] In addition there were nearly 800 works described as 'Black Letter books' including significant numbers of British and European incunabula. In particular the early works of the de Worde and Pynson presses are well represented. It was from these books and other collections that Martin was able to provide additional material for both Joseph Ames and William Herbert for their respective editions of the *Typographical Antiquities*.[41]

He was always ready to purchase manuscript collections or individual documents. One major acquisition was the purchase (possibly from

Blomefield's widow) of the 'innumerable letters of good consequence in history', which her husband had borrowed from the executors of the last Earl of Yarmouth,[42] and apparently never returned. These are of course now known to scholars as the Paston Letters. Another major manuscript acquired from Blomefield, although one which neither man recognised, was the earliest surviving manuscript of Sir Philip Sidney's *Defence of Poetry*, bound up with others in a volume entitled *Liber Miscellan*.[43]

Martin also continued to add large numbers of drawings, transcripts, letters and other loose papers to Le Neve's collections of these, as did Francis Blomefield during the periods he was using them. The majority were topographical or genealogical, although other packages contained notes of early printed books, and political, satirical and other verses. These last contain some examples of Martin's own poetry, including one poem in praise of drinking.[44] Also there is a most interesting short poem on the nature of intellectual freedom, transcribed from the 'bog wall' of one of the Inns of Court, although this may have been the work of Le Neve.

Martin was a regular participant in auctions in Norwich and elsewhere in East Anglia,[45] and often made purchases from booksellers in town and country.[46] He was also clearly attracted to the newly widowed. His extant papers show how he made extensive purchases not only from the surviving relicts of gentlemen collectors, such as Elizabeth Blomefield. He also made substantial purchases from the widows of deceased booksellers such as the widow of David Samuel of Kings Lynn, or of Mrs Barber of Thetford.[47] However, it should not be assumed that his contact with the bereaved was always purely for mercenary advantage. Martin seems to have spent months sorting Francis Blomefield's papers which 'were delivered to me in such wretched confusion that my pains have been unaccountable in sorting them out'.[48] Over the next decade he also went to considerable trouble to assist Blomefield's widow in disposing of the stocks of her husband's printed history.[49]

By 1753 Martin's reputation as a collector was such that his advice was sought by a certain Edward Holden over the disposal of 'a curious collection of pamphlets & manuscripts'.[50] They were described as 'the tedious labours of twenty years during the troublesome times of King Charles, containing many transactions as yet secret to the world'. As Holden wrote, 'I know well your taste and love of antiquity & curiosities and therefore pray you'll maturely consider how best and to whom an offer of such a fine collection shou'd be made'. Unfortunately Martin's reply has not been preserved, but given the ultimate fate of most of his library, perhaps it is as well that he did not have the resources to purchase the Thomason Tracts.

Administration of the library

Tom Martin, when sober, was an orderly man who loved arranging and classifying historical documents, who meticulously recorded all his book purchases. He also compiled many lists and catalogues of the different parts of his collections, such as 'Books in my library which relate to the antiquities and other curiosities of the city of Rome'[51] etc. etc.; but if there was any complete catalogue, it does not appear to have survived, although much of the collection can be pieced together from the five surviving sale catalogues compiled after his death.[52]

Unfortunately he has left little evidence of how he arranged his library, although there must have been bookcases throughout the house and those in his study contained his most prized possessions. There is a classification scheme for his substantial print collection, entitled 'The manner how my prints are plac'd in the Dining Room'.[53] This was an alphabetical system:

A	Antiques	K	Parliaments, Coronations, Funeralls
B	Scripture	L	General Maps
C	Beasts, Birds	M	Monies, Coins, Medals
D	Landskips	N	Deeds, Seals
E	Battles, Sieges	O	Deeds, Seals, Heads
F	Foreign Buildings	P	British Arms
G	Seals, Arms, Pedigrees, Foreign	Q	Knights of the Garter
H	Conversations, Still life	R	Miscellaneous
I	Hawking, Hunting, sports		

Then there was a gap in the scheme until:

X   Prints promiscuous (to be sorted)
Y   Duplicates to be exchang'd or sold
Z   Miscellaneous original drawings

There are also many records of his dealings with his bookbinders, in particular Samuel Harper. He was a countryman from the nearby village of Syleham, who appears to have trudged round the neighbourhood collecting 20 odd books at a time and returning them later. Martin used Harper's services for more than a decade and meticulously recorded every book as it was sent, and when it was returned.[54] He also recorded his purchases of binding materials, some of which survive. For example in March 1742/3 he asked the local carriers to purchase six rough calf and three pair sheep skins from Charles and Daniel Franklin, Leathersellers in Butchers Row

Temple Bar, which cost him seven shillings and three shillings respectively. At the same time he ordered six quire of marbled paper from Thomas Dowson, for seven shillings and six pence.[55]

Exploitation

The picture painted hitherto, of an orderly, but rather disreputable (if not dishonest) man does not explain the considerable affection and admiration in which he was held by two generations of English antiquaries. It does not explain why men such as Sir John Fenn (the editor of the Paston Letters), Sir John Cullum, Baronet, John Ives – the Suffolk Herald – and the topographer Richard Gough should go to considerable trouble and expense to perpetuate his memory.[56] The answer may be that Martin would always make available the resources of his library, and give unstintingly of his time to anyone interested in historical research. In a period when scholars outside London and the universities rarely had access to the materials they needed, correspondence with Martin could be a considerable asset.

Although he cannot be described as a historian, Martin's influence on contemporary historical writing was nevertheless considerable. His massive library was not the idle hobby of a rich man but was put to good use in assisting others. The names of a few of the antiquaries, historians, and numismatists of national repute whom Martin is known to have assisted include Browne Willis, Thomas Gale, William Cole, Andrew Ducarel, Sir Andrew Fountain, Joseph Ames, William Herbert, George Vertue, Richard Rawlinson, William Stukeley, Philip Carteret Webb, and Edward Rowe Mores.[57] Martin's correspondence with Andrew Ducarel also indicates that in 1755 and 1756 he went to considerable trouble to track down and retrieve some manuscripts on behalf of a Mr Franks of Pontefract. In particular he endeavoured to retrieve some valuable drawings that had been 'stuck upon the walls of a parson's necessary house'.[58]

Thus a good many of the books in the library were donations by their grateful authors. John Tanner, when sending a copy of his revision of his brother's *Notitia Monastica*, desired Martin 'should not speak of it lest every one whom he had any little assistance from should expect the same'.[59]

However, it was in his native East Anglia that Martin had the most noticeable influence on contemporary historiography. Tom Martin appears to have persuaded his neighbour Francis Blomefield to undertake the massive history of Norfolk based upon Le Neve's materials and provided him with every opportunity and assistance in using them. When Blomefield died in 1752, only part of the way through the job, it was Martin who went to considerable further trouble to persuade Charles Parkin to complete the work. Parkin also died before the history was published, and once again it appears to have been Martin who took pains to persuade the Kings Lynn bookseller, William Whittingham, to risk publishing the work.[60] Similarly Martin was active in assisting Henry Swinden to compile his history of Great Yarmouth, and earlier he corresponded with Benjamin Mackerell, the historian of King's Lynn and Norwich.[61] Towards the end of his life he assisted and corresponded with Philip Morant the historian of Essex, James Bentham the historian of Ely Cathedral, and Sir Joseph Ayloffe the would-be historian of Suffolk.[62]

Martin's library also appears to have been regarded as something of a tourist attraction among the learned who happened to be visiting East Anglia, who would also be sure to benefit from his hospitality. The engraver and antiquary George Vertue has left an account of one such brief visit in 1739:

From thence wee went to see Thom: Martin at Palgrave brother Antiquary – who entertained us with much Friendly civility. his Collections are very curious and valuable his pictures &c. Armes grants Chartularies Mss. of many kinds great collections towards the History of Suffolk & Norfolk. some rare old printed books. this collection & his own collections of Notes & remarkable deeds is very numerous. and woud require much time to consider well. all the time wee had there that evening & next morning was fully employed, to see and cursorily observe what was possible in our short stay.[62]

The fate of the library

Martin ought not to have been a poor man. He had a reasonable inheritance, his income as an attorney, the considerable assets brought by each of his wives, and later legacies from his brother. Yet he did not have the financial resources to maintain his chosen style of living. As Sir John Cullum described it:

Mr. Martin's desire was not only to be esteemed, but to be known and distinguished by the name of Honest Tom Martin of Palgrave, an ambition in which his acquaintance saw no reason not to gratify him. ... Had he desired the appellation of wise and prudent, his inattention to his business, his contempt and improper use of money, and his fondness for mixed and festive company, would have debarred him, as the father of a numerous family, of that pretension. He died poor, having been little attentive to frugality and sobriety; but left behind him the character of an honest man.[64]

By 1762 his profligate life-style and obsessional book-collecting eventually caught up with him. In April of that year Andrew Ducarel, the librarian at Lambeth Palace, received a sorry account from his friend in Palgrave blaming everybody else for his troubles except their true author.

My eldest son has married very imprudently; that daughter .. now is, and for two years, past has been, confined, through a high disorder in her senses, without any present symptoms of ever recovering. My second son (whom I had bound out to a Surgeon and Apothecary) enlisted for a common soldier. Others in my family, either afflicted with sickness, or not behaving with that dutifulness, as to be any company in my old age. &c &c. And, to complete my calamities fortune has seemed for a long while past to frown upon me. Pardon me, my dear friend, for troubling you with this ungrateful detail of my misfortune, but, in short, they have brought me under a necessity of parting with my large and expensive Collection of Books, Deeds, Coins, and various other Curiosities, in my life-time. Nor do I repine at it, as I have no child who understands any thing about them. The great hardship is the present scarcity of money, and want of friends to advise and direct me in what method to dispose of them to the best advantage. Sometimes I am thinking of finding out some Nobleman or Gentleman who would purchase them all together; sometimes of offering the most choice of them to the British Museum; and at other times of exposing them to a public sale or auction in town.[65]

This letter marks the beginning of the end of the collection. Ducarel replied giving his advice and commiseration:-

Drs Commons May 4 1762
My good friend
   I received your kind letter of the 25th April on Friday last – It has given me an infinite concern; & the series of Misfortunes which seem at once, to overwhelm you, will I hope, thro' gods blessing, daily decrease; & to enjoy a good state of health, at this particular time, is a peculiar Happiness from heaven – As I have no connexions in Suffolk all you mentioned was entirely new to me & as to your daughter, who lived in London, I had neither seen nor heard any thing about her for upwards of two years–
   The best advice I can give you, you are welcome to – & since you are now under a necessity of parting with your large & expensive collection, the business is, to do it in the most advantageous manner – For that purpose I have this day consulted with our old friend Dr Birch – & we both agree first that the best way will be to dispose of the whole collection by auction & recommend Baker the Bookseller as the properest person to be employed in the management thereof.
   As to ye Books – We both agree 2dly that Baker is the fittest person to make a Catalogue of them & the Mss. & to dispose them properly.
   3dly As to ye old deeds Chartae &c &c &c we both agree that Baker is not a proper person to make a Catalogue of them – but that your self should draw up a list

or account of them, Which you can easily do; as, we apprehend, they are digested according to their counties –

4thly We both agree that we do not know any nobleman or Gentleman now in this kingdom who would purchase the whole collection of chartae &c together – & that even if such a Nobleman could be found it would be almost impossible to find persons, properly qualified, to set a true value & Estimation of them between the buyer & the seller.

5thly We both agree that if these are put up to auction, in parcells according to the Counties, they will fetch a much greater price by that means than by any other.

6thly We both agree that the list or Catalogue of the old Deeds &c should be published a month, at least, before the Auction begins that Gentlemen might be apprized, in time, of what they are.

7thly We both think it not improbable that Baker will advance money upon the Collection; when in his hands but that he will confine himself to the Books & Mss only, as to the Loan of money...[66]

The bookseller referred to is, of course, Samuel Baker of York Street, the founder of Sotheby's, who specialised in antiquarian book auctions.

Ducarel also undertook to approach the Archbishop to see whether he would be prepared to buy any of his friend's manuscripts relating to the See of Canterbury. However, when it came to it Martin simply could not bring himself to sell more books than he needed to meet his immediate debts. The next nine years therefore saw a gradual selling of books and manuscripts as creditors became so pressing that they could no longer be ignored. He hated parting with any book, describing it as 'driving the first nail in his coffin'.[67] He listed several hundred books in a document which he later endorsed 'These I once intended to have parted with but now have taken those with this mark into my study.'[68] Over half of the books have been so marked.

1763 saw the sale of the valuable collection of gold and silver medals to Lord Maynard.[69] By 1768 his situation was again so bad that he was forced to invite the London bookseller Thomas Payne to visit Palgrave and make him an offer for whatever books he would. (This bookseller was incidentally described by John Nichols as 'Honest Tom Payne').[70] John Fenn has a pathetic account of this period:

Whilst Mr Payne was examining his library and picking out such books as he thought proper, Mr Martin would never come near him, though often in a morning early, whilst every one else was in bed, he would get up, go down into his library, take away and hide up such old curious books as he most valued. Many of these were found after his death hidden in various parts of the house.[71]

Epilogue

Martin died in March 1771 a sorely disappointed man. Almost to the end he would assist anyone who applied to him for information from his library, even though he knew he would not live to see the results of such labours in print.[72] Not surprisingly, his widow had no great attachment to the books and manuscripts which had dominated her life through two marriages and ensured their old age was lived in poverty. She immediately let it be known that she was going to dispose of the collection largely for the benefit of her husband's creditors. Over the next few months she sold many of the most choice items to antiquarian friends of her husband's such as John Fenn and John Ives and other private collectors. It was probably at this time that John Fenn acquired the Paston Letters, which he later published.

The complete dispersal of Martin's remaining library took place over the next seven or eight years. It was as though destiny were conspiring to remove all traces of this illegitimate collection as quickly as possible.[73] The bookseller William Whittingham of King's Lynn, who had collaborated with Martin in the publication of the remaining parts of Blomefield's *History* was called in to make an overall appraisal of the remaining collections.[74] These were then sold to John Worth, a Diss Chemist, and Fellow of the Society of Antiquaries, for £660, a fraction of their true value. Worth quickly auctioned off the pictures, prints, ancient weapons and so on in Diss. He also sold many manuscripts directly to John Ives. Then, in 1773, the printed books were sold *en masse* to the Norwich booksellers Booth and Berry for £330. They in turn sold large numbers by weight in Diss and then removed about 6,000 to Norwich, where they were disposed of in a marked catalogue priced at more than £2,000. Most of the remaining manuscripts were auctioned by what had become the firm of Baker and Leigh in London, in April 1773 and May 1774, and raised a further £450.

John Worth also intended to publish Martin's long-expected account of Thetford. He advertised the work, commissioned some engravings and a few sheets were printed in Norwich; but shortly afterwards, in December 1774, he too died insolvent.[75] All that remained of Martin's collections were then purchased by Mr Hunt, bookseller, at Harleston, who incorporated them into a marked catalogue, and sold the rest to private purchasers.[76] The dispersal was completed by the premature death of John Ives and the dispersal of his collection in London, in March 1777. All that remained of the collection at the end was the many bundles of loose papers originally compiled by Le Neve, which eventually Sir John Fenn agreed to take, merely to save them from destruction. Most of them now exist in the Norfolk Record Office, and although they are a gold mine for 17th- and 18th-century history, they are a nightmare to use.

Martin's friends did not forget him. Sir John Fenn read a paper about Martin to the Society of Antiquaries, and subsequently left money for a monument to his memory in Palgrave church.[78] In 1772 John Ives wrote and privately printed an elegy on the death of his friend, and also paid for an engraved portrait of him.[79] Finally Richard Gough bought up the notes and some plates of the History of Thetford from Hunt, and published the work, incorporating Sir John Cullum's account of the author.

According to Fenn, Tom Martin was:

A friendly and cheerful neighbour, and when sober, an instructive and entertaining companion; and would he have paid that attention to his profession that his abilities enabled him to do, and which circumstances and children required he should do, he might have possessed such a fortune as would have entitled him both to have pursued his favourite amusements with comfort and satisfaction, and to have provided for his family; but being always distressed, his mind was uneasy, and he too often sought relief from low company.[80]

Dibdin's assessment was

Martin's book pursuits were miscellaneous, and perhaps a little too wildly followed up; yet some good fortune contributed to furnish his collection with volumes of singular curiosity.[81]

Much of Ives's *Pastoral elegy* is rather amateurish, and not worth preserving, although four verses do perhaps contribute to the picture of the man.

Strephon
Antiquity in him her Champion lost;
Of all her votaries few with him compared:
Her relicts purchased at the dearest cost:
Others with him the curious pleasure shared.

Damon
With fixt contempt he viewed the gilded Ore,
Which holds so many thousands in its chains:
Few will in search of knowledge make them poor
We'll hope the pleasure paid him for his pains.

Strephon
And sure it did for goodness ruled his heart;
Complacency was seated in his breast;

Honor and Probity, held each a part.
And Honesty composed his Soul to rest.

Damon
His lively sallies shewed a chearfull mind –
On goodness chearfullness will sure attend:
Yet did his Wit oft leave a sting behind
For not exempt from faults was this our Friend.

The closing verse would also make an appropriate epitaph, to this singular, if misguided book collector:

Strephon
Oh! Sight of woe! – sad, sable, awfull, slow:
Grim Death, thy power disown, what mortal can?
The victim thou has summon'd, Tyrant know,
Now sleeps at peace – he was – *an Honest Man.*

References

1. Thomas F. Dibdin, *Bibliomania* (London: Chatto & Windus, 1876), p.384. William Younger Fletcher, *English book collectors* (New York: Burt Franklin, 1902), p.148, and Seymour De Ricci, *English collectors of books & manuscripts (1530-1930) and their marks of ownership* (Cambridge University Press, 1930), pp.65, 68.
2. The best sources for Martin's early life are the account taken from his own notes in his *History of Thetford* ed. R. Gough (London: J. Nichols, 1779), pp.284-5 and the memoir of Martin by Sir John Cullum which was prefixed to this work (pp.xi-xviii). In addition Sir John Fenn prepared 'Memoirs of the life of Thomas Martin, Gent.,' which were read to the Society of Antiquaries on 23rd November 1780, and which he subsequently enlarged in 1784. These were not, however, published until 1904 (*Norfolk Archaeology*, XV. (1904), pp.233-48). There are also accounts of Martin in *DNB*, and John Nichols, *Literary Anecdotes of the Eighteenth Century*, 9 vols (London: J. Nichols, 1812-15), V, pp.384-9, but these are derived from the earlier sources.
3. His father was William Martin, rector of Great Livermore and Curate of St Mary's Thetford.
4. His mother was Elizabeth Burrough, aunt of Sir James Burrough, subsequently master of Caius College.
5. British Library Add. MS 5876, f.88.
6. B.L. Add. MS 5833, f.166.
7. Fenn, *Memoirs*, p.246.
8. Fenn, *Memoirs*, p.241.
9. Cullum (see note 2).
10. For example, Norfolk Record Office, Norfolk and Norwich Archaeological Society Deposit, NNAS c3/2/5 contains large numbers of Martin's transcripts and facsimiles of Elizabethan deeds. Martin's papers are now widely dispersed among manuscript

collections, although the majority of Martin's are in the Norfolk Record Office. The two main sources are the Frere Manuscripts, and the Norfolk & Norwich Archaeological Society Deposit (both collections are largely uncatalogued). Other materials are to be found in the Duleep Singh Deposit, Castle Museum Deposit, and Colman Manuscripts. There are also surviving manuscripts in the Suffolk Record Office, the British Library, among the Gough Manuscripts in the Bodleian Library, Arundel Castle and also probably in collections overseas.

11. Letter to Samuel Kerrich, rector of Dersingham 13 December 1737 (N.R.O. NNAS c3/1/9, f.20).

12. The origin of Martin's sobriquet is discussed by Fenn (246), and is said to date from its mysterious appearance on the subscription list for Zachary Grey's *Hudibras* in 1744. However it is clear from the previous reference that its use predates this by at least seven years.

13. He was admitted Fellow in 1718 on the recommendation of Peter Le Neve, President of the Society. He also later became a member of the Gentleman's Society of Spalding.

14. Letter to Beaupré Bell 27 December 1734 (N.R.O. Rye Ms. 32, f.28).

15. Many of these are listed in Thomas Worth's *A catalogue of the entire collection of prints, coins, &c &c. Of the late Mr Martin F.A.S. which will be sold by Auction at the King's-Head of Diss Norfolk on Thursday the 29th and Friday the 30th and Saturday the 31st October and Monday the 2nd November 1772* ([London?], 1772).

16. Letter to Andrew Ducarel 25 May 1762. N.R.O. NNAS C.3/1/5.

17. Letter to John Tanner 27 July 1743, in Nichols, *Literary Anecdotes*, XI, p.413. Blomefield noted in his *A History of the Ancient City and Burgh of Thetford* (Fersfield: 1739) that a fuller account was expected from his friend Thomas Martin.

18. John Fenn wrote to Richard Gough in 1777 'The Thetford History was compiled from Mr Martin's papers, in Mr Worth's possession, by a Mr Davis dissenting minister, who lived at Diss'. However, according to Richard Gough's preface to the work, he 'bought the manuscript, with the undigested materials, copy-right, and plates. The first of these required a general revisal..' and he is therefore usually listed as the editor. John Nichols, *Illustrations of the Literary History of the Eighteenth Century*, 8 vols. (London: J. Nichols, 1817-58). V, pp.167-8.

19. N.R.O. NNAS c3/2/10.

20. Fenn, *Memoirs*, p.236.

21. N.R.O. NNAS c3/2/11.

22. Nichols, *Literary Anecdotes*, V, p.385.

23. Fenn, pp.238-9.

24. Many of these are preserved in N.R.O. NNAS c3/2/11.

25. Suffolk Record Office (a microfilm copy is also held by the N.R.O. MF/RO 410/1).

26. See Patrick and Felicity Strong, 'The last will and codicils of Henry V', *English Historical Review*, XCVI, 1981, pp.79-101. William Cole also recorded this event (B.L. Add. MS 5841 f.2). B.L. Add. MSS 24318-9 include a copy of Martin's digest of the records and his 'Collections out of the Chapell & Muniment room at Eton College'.

27. Richard Gough, *British Topography* (London: 2 vols., 1780), II, p.2.

28. This collection is described in more detail in Diarmaid MacCulloch, *The Chorography of Suffolk*, Suffolk Record Society XIX (1976), 1-4, and David Stoker 'The Compilation and Production of a Classic County History' (unpublished M.Phil thesis, University of Reading, 1982).

29. Nichols, *Illustrations of the Literary History*, III, p.433.

30. Public Record Office, Prerogative Court of Canterbury Wills. 1729, No.633 and George Stephen, *Three Centuries of a City Library* (Norwich: 1917), pp.24-5.

31. *A Catalogue of the Valuable Library Collected by that truly laborious Antiquary, Peter Le Neve, Esq.; Norroy King of Arms... Which will be sold by Auction the 22nd Day of February 1730-1 at the Bedford Coffee-house... By John Wilcox, Bookseller.*

32. Fenn, *Memoirs*, p.239.

33. Letter from Thomas Tanner to Francis Blomefield 22 October 1733. N.R.O. Rye Ms.32, ff.10-11.

34. Letter from Thomas Tanner to Richard Rawlinson 2 October 1735 (Bodleian Library Rawlinson Letters 30, f.31).

35. See note 32.

36. Letter from Francis Blomefield to John Tanner, 2 January 1735/6 (N.R.O. Rye Ms. 32, f.65).

37. Francis Blomefield, *An Essay towards a Topographical History of Norfolk*, 5 vols. (Fersfield, Norwich, Lynn: 1739-75), I, Introduction.

38. Letter from Francis Blomefield to Henry Briggs 4 January 1734/4 (N.R.O. Rye Ms. 32, ff.28-9).

39. Nichols, *Literary Anecdotes*, IX, p.419.

40. *Bibliotheca Martiniana: a Catalogue of the Entire Library of the late eminent Antiquary Mr Thomas Martin... which will be sold ... by Martin Booth and John Berry* [Norwich?: 1772].

41. N.R.O. NNAS c3/2/1 includes a large envelope including a book cover entitled *Typographical Antiquities*. Within this are several hundred slips compiled by Martin and John Fenn of books missing from Ames's edition of this work (London: 1749), notes of which were apparently supplied to William Herbert in preparation for the second edition (3 vols., 1785-90). See also John Fenn's letters to Herbert, Nichols, *Illustrations of the Literary History*, V, pp.168-70.

42. Blomefield's discovery of these letters was mentioned in a letter from him to Major Weldon (Sir William Paston's executor) 13 May 1735 (N.R.O. Rye Ms. 32, fo.33). They do not however appear in either a receipt for manuscripts taken by Martin from Mrs Blomefield in September 1752 or else a list of manuscripts purchased from her in 1753 (both N.R.O. NNAS c3/2/10). It is possible therefore that they may have been acquired by Martin before Blomefield's death.

43. Mary Mahl, 'A treatise of horsman shipp', *Times Literary Supplement*, 21 December 1967, p.1245.

44. NRO NNAS c3/1/12 'Collections of political satirical amorous and miscellaneous verses of varying merit and length made by Peter Le Neve and Thomas Martin'.

45. For example he made purchases at Auditor Jett's auction, 1730, at Corbett's Auction February 1732, the Reverend Mr Pykarell's sale 1739, and Oswald's sale February 1740 (N.R.O. NNAS c3/2/11).

46. These included Mr Marshall, Woodbridge,1745/6, Mr Gleed, Norwich 1741/2, Mr Jones, Cockey Lane Norwich 1731 (who is not otherwise known as a bookseller), Fletcher Gyles, London 1740, and various other unspecified booksellers in London and Winchester, 1740 (N.R.O. NNAS c3/2/11).

47. Lists of books purchased 1720-1 and 1745 respectively survive in N.R.O. NNAS c3/2/11. In other cases it is not clear whether the purchases made were from members of the book trade or private individuals.

48. Letter from Martin to Nehemiah Lodge April 1755 (N.R.O. Ms.453). N.R.O. NNAS

c3/2/10 contains various priced lists of Blomefield's books and manuscripts including a list of purchases by Martin. Martin's and Charles Parkin's attempts at assisting Blomefield's widow are also recorded in letters between them N.R.O. NNAS c3/2/10, and in various memoranda, Bodl. Lib. Ms.Top.Gen.c102.

49. Letter to Andrew Ducarel July 10, 1765 (Nichols, *Literary Anecdotes*, IX), p.426.
50. N.R.O. NNAS c3/2/11.
51. Ibid.
52. These are: *A Catalogue of the Library of Mr Thomas Martin of Palgrave in Suffolk, lately deceased* (Lynn: 1772) ESTC t098426; *A Catalogue of the Entire Collection of Prints, Coins, &c &c. Of the late Mr Martin F.A.S.* (see Note 14); *Bibliotheca Martiniana: a catalogue of the library of the late eminent antiquary Mr Thomas Martin, ... Which will be sold ...Saturday June 5, by Martin Booth and John Berry*, ([Norwich], 1773) ESTC t098426; *A catalogue of the very Curious, Valuable, and Numerous Collection of manuscripts of Thomas Martin ... which will be sold by Auction, by S. Baker and G. Leigh, ... on Wednesday, April 28, 1773, ...* [London, 1773], and *A catalogue of the Remaining Part of the Library of the Late Well known Antiquary Mr. Martin.... Which will be sold, by Auction, by S. Baker and G. Leigh, ... on Wednesday the 18th of May 1774* [London: 1774].
53. N.R.O. NNAS c3/2/11.
54. Martin regularly used the services of Samuel Harper from about January 1743 until the mid 1750s, making two copies of each record of books, one of which he retained. The other was subsequently returned containing the prices (NNAS c3/2/11).
55. Other binders used include Mr Reason, February 1738/9 (presumably W. Reason of London) and Mrs Watson, April 1742 [of Bury St Edmunds] (NNAS c3/2/11).
56. Fenn and Cullum both wrote memoirs of Martin (see note 2). Ives subscribed for an engraved plate, and Gough edited Martin's notes.
57. All of these men either corresponded with Martin or else are mentioned in his correspondence.
58. N.R.O. NNAS c3/1/5, and Nichols, *Literary Anecdotes*, IX, p.416.
59. Nichols, *Illustrations of Literature*, V, p.436.
60. See David Stoker, 'Mr Parkin's magpie, the other Mr Whittingham, and the fate of Great Yarmouth', *The Library*, 6th ser., XII, 1990, pp.121-31. Parkin also gave Martin a copy of his *An impartial account of the Invasion under William Duke of Normandy* (London, 1756) which he had published 'out of pure love of old England, and to animate us all against any French invasion' (N.R.O. NNAS c3/2/4).
61. Nichols, *Literary Anecdotes*, IX, p.428, and a letter from Mackerell to Francis Blomefield 17 October 1735 (N.R.O. Rye Ms. 32, f.46).
62. Nichols, *Literary Anecdotes*, IX, pp.413-29.
63. *Vertue Note Books*, V. (Oxford, 1938). Walpole Society. 26, p.119.
64. See note 2.
65. Nichols, *Literary Anecdotes*, IX, pp.420-1.
66. N.R.O., NNAS c3/1/5.
67. Fenn, *Memoirs*, 245, and John Chambers, *A general history of the county of Norfolk* (Norwich: 2 vols., 1829), II, p.914.
68. N.R.O. NNAS c3/2/11.
69. Fenn wrote 'an account of the disposal and total dispersion of Mr Martin's various collections' to accompany his 'Memoir', *Norfolk Archaeology*, XV (1904), pp.249-66.
70. Nichols, *Literary Anecdotes*, VI, p.440.

71. Fenn, *Memoirs*, p.245.
72. Nichols, *Literary Anecdotes*, IX, p.428-9.
73. For a detailed (although not entirely complete) account of the sale, see Fenn, 'An account of the disposal...', pp.249-66.
74. N.R.O. NNAS c3/2/12. 'Mr Whittingham's appraisement of Mr Thomas Martin's Library, 1771' and *A catalogue of the library of Mr Thomas Martin of Palgrave in Suffolk, lately deceased* (Lynn: W. Whittingham, 1772), ESTC t098426.
75. *Proposals for printing by subscription the history of the town of Thetford, ... compiled from the papers of the late well-known antiquary, Mr Thomas Martin. By John Worth, F.A.S.* [Norwich: John Crouse, 1774] (a copy is in the Norwich Public Library).
76. Fenn's letters to Richard Gough regarding the purchase of the remaining materials from Hunt are published in Nichols, *Illustrations of the literary history*, V, pp.167-8.
77. Most of this collection now constitutes the Frere Manuscripts, but other significant parts are preserved in the Duleep Singh collection and Norfolk and Norwich Antiquarian Society Manuscripts.
78. See note 2, and the *DNB* entry for Martin. John Ives had intended to erect such a monument, but had died unexpectedly before he did so, see Cullum's preface to Martin's *History of Thetford*.
79. John Ives, *A pastoral elegy on the death of Thomas Martin of Palgrave in Suffolk* (Yarmouth: John Ives, 1772). One copy survives in N.R.O. NNAS c3/2/12.
80. Fenn, 'Memoirs,' pp.248-9.
81. Dibdin, *Bibliomania*, pp.384-6.

Reading as Pastime: the place of light literature in some gentlemen's libraries of the 17th century

T.A. BIRRELL

Some preliminary definitions

THIS PAPER is concerned with reading, not collecting. If a man buys a book for any other purpose than reading it, or intending to read it, he is a collector, not a reader. Some of the libraries that will be referred to are very large, but their owners were readers, not collectors.

'Gentlemen', for present purposes, includes professional men, civil servants, and country gentlemen, and goes right up the social scale. But all clergymen and all academics will be excluded – the inhabitants of Oxford and Cambridge are, on the whole, not truly representative of the phenomena to be described.

The importance of light literature in the study of gentry reading habits

There is an almost total lack of studies of 17th-century readership in England from the consumer angle. There are of course several studies of readership from the production angle: what was on the market. H.S. Bennett's three volume *English Books and Readers 1475-1640* (Cambridge 1952-70) is the standard work. But what we want now is English Readers and Books – a very different thing. To be sure, we have Margaret Spufford, *Small Books and Pleasant Histories. Popular Fiction and its Readership in the 17th Century* (Cambridge 1984), which attempts to describe 'the mental world of the peasant reader'. Dr Spufford bases her study on the late 17th-century collection of popular black letter tracts in the Pepysian library. The really interesting social and cultural point, surely, is not that the peasants read such stuff – they would, wouldn't they? What is interesting about 17th-century culture is that a high ranking civil servant like Pepys bought and read such stuff for his evident pleasure. 17th-century culture is essentially a culture where reading habits are not stratified into peasant, bourgeois and gentry – gentry reading tastes were inclusive, and included the tastes of the peasants and the bourgeois. After all, the surviving copies of very rare popular and bourgeois books that are in our research libraries today have virtually all ultimately come from 17th-century gentry libraries.

The contents of the 17th-century gentleman's library was of course predominantly utilitarian: he bought the books he needed. As a landowner and magistrate he needed books on law. As a patron of church livings he needed books on theology. His interest in local history was largely a landowner's interest. General history was ethics: you learnt from the past how to behave in the world to your own best advantage. And even the acquisition of literature, belles lettres, was partly utilitarian. It was justified as a mixture of the *utile* and the *dulce*. The classical concept *utile dulce* was recycled for the benefit of the puritanly inclined by Sir Philip Sidney, the head prefect of the English Renaissance. The object of poesie, that is fiction, is, he says, 'to teach goodness and delight the learners'. Sir Edward Coke, in his library catalogue, prefaces the section on poetry with the words 'and seeing that *et prodesse solent et delectare poete*, in the next place shall follow books of poetrie'.[1] Coke knew full well that it was manors, as well as manners, that maketh man.

This paper, therefore, focuses on reading as a pastime, without any motive of profit, moral or otherwise. The characteristic of the leisure class, as defined by Thorstein Veblen, is conspicuous waste. One thing they could waste was time, and they could waste time by reading books that were primarily time-killers. Such books fall into three categories: plays, novels, and miscellanies (that is, *facetiae*, burlesques and *joco-seria*).

A striking feature of gentry libraries is the collections, one might almost say systematic runs, of quarto plays. Well-known examples are the play collections of Thomas Mostyn of Mostyn Hall, and of Sir Richard Newdigate of Arbury, and also the Harington and Oxinden Collections.[2] Less well known are the collections of Edward 2nd Viscount Conway and of Ralph Sheldon of Beoley, who died in 1684. Sheldon's library was auctioned in the 18th century by Christie and Ansell.[3] Lot 523 consisted of Shakespeare's first folio, Milton's *Paradise Lost*, and one other. Christie's cataloguers have come on a bit since then. What is really interesting is lot 422, consisting of 56 bound quarto volumes of 'scarce old plays by various authors'. Assuming ten plays to a volume, that would come to 560 plays, before 1684.

Plays were acquired on a systematic scale that would be unthinkable in a non-specialist private library today. Men like Mostyn, Newdigate, Conway and Sheldon simply acquired every play that they could lay their hands on.[4] The implication is, therefore, that plays were read as the most accessible form of fiction. The acquisition of plays in the 17th century was the equivalent of subscribing to *All the Year Round* in the 19th century, or to the *Strand Magazine* in the 20th century. Play reading, as distinct from play going, was a separate and important cultural activity.[5] Quarto plays were not records of performance, they were fictions in their own right, and they were read as stories, for the plot.

Where you find the drama, there you will usually find the novel. The novel does not begin in the 18th century with Richardson and Fielding: there was prose fiction long before that, however dreary it may seem to the modern reader, who wants the novel to provide psychological and sociological insights, and not just an adventure story or a plot. It is characteristic of the 17th-century gentry library that it includes Greek, Latin, Italian, Spanish and French novels indiscriminately mixed with English novels. It may be more usual to talk of them as romances: pastoral, heroic, parodic or picaresque. They are all fiction, to be read to pass the time, and as fiction the novel is closely linked, in 17th-century literary culture, to the drama. All the evidence of library catalogues points to the fact that where a gentleman has plenty of English drama, he also has the continental sources and analogues from which the plots of that drama are derived.[6] Sir Henry Thomas was quite wrong in his estimate of the reception in England of Spanish romances: 'in general their appeal was to the lower, or at least the ignorant, classes'.[7] In fact, the gentry not only possessed the texts of the chivalric romances in Spanish, Italian and French, they also possessed the English versions as well.

The third class of gentry light reading – miscellanies, facetiae, nugae, *joco-seria* – could be called 'popular' in two senses of the word. English jest books, riddles and maxims are obviously 'popular' in the sense of appealing to the 'lower' classes – but the gentry have not only the English variety but also the Latin, French and Italian versions of the genre as well. Furthermore, they have a kind of reading-matter which could only have been 'popular' within their own class: the sort of books which qualify as upper-class or sophisticated time-wasting – something which might appeal to the sort of mentality which today does the *Times* Crossword, or listens to Round Britain Quiz.

The *New Cambridge Bibliography*[8] gets the two kinds of 'popular' literature mixed up, but the subject catalogue of the *Bibliothèque du Roi* (Paris 1750) is clearer. It puts the sophisticated miscellaneous category as a subsection of the general heading of novels and romances. The main subheading is *Facéties, pièces burlesques*. This is further subdivided into 'Ouvrages badins sur toutes sortes de matières', then 'Ouvrages badins sur les matières de Jurisprudence, d'Histoire, de Philosophie, et de Belles Lettres', and finally 'Ouvrages licencieux', which means pornography. Facetious, burlesque, jocular, waggish, bantering: this is a category which is especially worth looking for in 17th-century gentlemen's libraries. Some of it is ambiguously presented to appeal to the moralistic market, and so you get the category of *joco-seria*. Within the genre come the books that derive from the Erasmian tradition of the *Adagia, Colloquia* and *Encomia*.[9] By the mid-17th century this includes 'paradoxes': after Erasmus's *Praise of Folly*, you have the praise of baldness, of blindness, of gout, and so on. Then there are certain types of essays: not the Essays of Bacon or Montaigne, they are ethics – but the frivolous essays of Sir William Cornwallis, who wrote In Praise of the French Pox, In Praise of Julian the Apostate's Virtues, and In Praise of Nothing. Charles Lamb was not the inventor of the trivial essay.

Also within the genre are epigrams in the tradition of Martial: the obvious examples are Owen's *Epigrams* and the degenerate versions of Owen, all of which, in English as well as Latin, enjoyed a great success. Then there is satire and burlesque: not Juvenalian satire, which is moral, but the Lucianic and Menippean tradition, which is satire just for the hell of it. Then the character writers: not Theophrastus himself, who comes under morals or ethics, but Overbury, Earle and John Stephens, which are burlesque. Then the debates: on drink, on tobacco or on women. Here the ambiguity of the appeal is most manifest – you can take them seriously or you can take them as burlesque.[10]

The genre of the miscellany, and its sub-genres, may be defined and described in various ways: it testifies to a genuine upper-class taste for reading time-wasting rubbish in all languages. The English purveyors of this sort of literature have never been studied as a group, or as a distinct cultural phenomenon. There is, however, one example familiar to most literary students: the title-page of the 1652 edition of Donne's *Paradoxes* (see illustration). When John Donne Junior wanted to market his late father's bits and pieces, he dressed it up to look like a miscellany volume: Paradoxes, Problemes (for the *Times* Crossword mentality), Essayes (carefully omitting to mention that most of them were essays in divinity), Characters, Epigrams (written in Latin and translated into English, to cater for classicists and non-classicists) and Ignatius his Conclave, A Satyr (Menippean of course). Donne Junior, and his publisher Humphrey Moseley, clearly wanted the gentry to believe that this book was wholly frivolous: they were presenting the late Dean of St Paul's *en pantoufles*.

The interpretation of private library catalogues

There is an extensive literature on how to describe a book, but there is no literature whatever on how to describe a library or a library catalogue. A

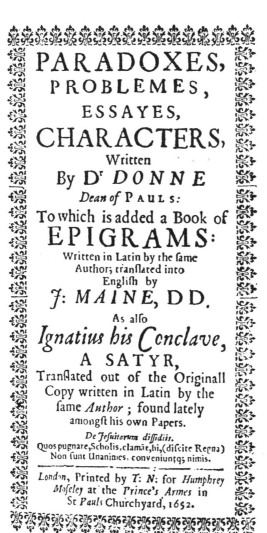

PARADOXES,
PROBLEMES,
ESSAYES,
CHARACTERS,
Written

By Dr *DONNE*

Dean of PAULS:

To which is added a Book of
EPIGRAMS:
Written in Latin by the fame
Author; tranflated into
Englifh by
J: *MAINE*, DD.

As alfo

Ignatius his Conclave,

A SATYR,

Tranflated out of the Originall
Copy written in Latin by the
fame *Author* ; found lately
amongft his own Papers.

De Jefuitarum diffidiis.
Quos pugnare, Scholis, clamát, hi, (difcite Regna)
Non funt Unanimes, conveniuntq; nimis.

London, Printed by *T*: *N*: for *Humphrey*
Moseley at the *Prince's Armes* in
St *Pauls* Churchyard, 1652.

private library is part of its owner's biography: the known facts of his life may help in the understanding of his choice of books. But the converse may also be true: his choice of books may add to the understanding of the known facts of his life – and for this purpose a purely statistical analysis of the contents of his library is inadequate. For instance, the puritan radical, John Webster of Clitheroe (1611-82) was a clergyman, a surgeon, a metallurgist, a linguist, and an educational reformer: his library reflects all the hitherto known aspects of his *persona*. But what sticks out like a sore thumb is his extensive collection of romances, obviously part of a deliberate acquisitions policy: it was the nearest a puritan could get to a collection of 'curiosa'.[11]

If therefore the interpretation of a private library is to be of any real use for the study of individual reading habits, it has to be deliberately impressionistic: the particularities have to take precedence over the generalities. The book-historian has, unashamedly, to play his hunches – which means that he has to decide what are the oddities in a collection, and then of course to read them. The following notes on a few unfamiliar catalogues of 17th-century gentry libraries are intended to illustrate the use of a non-systematic approach as an aid to the study of reading habits, as well as to support the general thesis of this paper.

WILLIAM PAGET, 4TH LORD PAGET OF BEAUDESERT (1572-1628)
William Paget's father, Thomas 3rd Lord Paget, had been implicated in plots against Elizabeth I, fled abroad in 1583, and was deprived of his title and estates. William Paget, from the age of eleven, had been brought up as a ward of court. He went on the expedition to Cadiz in 1596 (what young aristocrat did not?), served in the Paris embassy in 1598, and was on the Council of the Virginia Company. His library was catalogued in 1617 by John Hassall (B.L.Harl.MS 3267) and consists of about 1,600 books, arranged under subjects. It includes books in French, Italian, Spanish, Latin and Greek, and there are also grammars and dictionaries of Hebrew and German. The largest section is Theology, 385 volumes (75% Protestant and 25% Roman Catholic). Then comes History, 335 volumes, Philosophy 210, Mathematics 178 (including Music, Architecture and Painting), Law 70, Military 70, Medicine and Chemistry 63, Poetry 63, Logic 45, Letterwriters 35, and 78 volumes under the heading 'Variarum rerum sive promiscuae doctrinae scriptores', i.e. Various.

At first sight, it seems to contain no plays and no romances, and only 63 volumes of poetry, but whoever the cataloguer John Hassall may have been, he had a very peculiar idea of subject classification. Boccaccio and Rabelais are under history, and so too are the romances of the Chevalier

Bayard and Heliodorus. The pastoral romances of Longus and others, and the *novelle* of Sansovino are classified as various and the *Lettere amorose* of Sansovino and Pasqualigo are under letter-writers. But it is under 'various' that we shall find most of the *facetiae* or *joco-seria*. Paget has Lucian in the original Greek and, in Latin, Petronius, Barclay's *Euphormio* and the *opuscula* of Thomas More. In Italian he has the *facetiae* of Domenichi and Zabata, and in French the *Satyre Menippée* and *Les Bigarrures* of Des Accords (Etienne Tabourot). *Les Bigarrures* (the medleys or miscellanies) was an immensely popular book in the gentry libraries of the 17th century. It is a small manual on acrostics, anagrams, chronograms, strange verse forms and numerology, together with examples of the various genres. It seems to have been almost a basic handbook for the study of poetics, yet it is never mentioned in academic studies of Anglo-French literary relations.[12] In English, Paget has the weird book of Thomas Lupton, *A Thousand Notable Things of Sundry Sortes* (six editions before 1617), which is a collection of fantastic medical recipes intermingled with tall tales. The character books of Overbury, Breton and John Stephens are classified as philosophy, and Dekker's *Belman of London* is classed as history.

William Paget's library illustrates two points. First, never trust 17th-century subject categories, and secondly, even in a fundamentally serious library, you will nearly always find an element of light and frivolous reading if you really look for it.

Scipio Le Squyer (1579-1659)
In the Elizabethan Club at Yale there is a copy of the first quarto of Shakespeare's *Pericles* (1609), inscribed 'Scipio Le Squyer 15 May 1609'. In his preface to the Elizabethan Club Catalogue, Alan Bell writes: 'One would have liked to know so much more of the books, reading habits and theatrical interests of the Scipio Le Squyer who wrote his name and the date... on the titlepage of the 1609 *Pericles*'. Two minutes with Sears Jayne's *Library Catalogues of the English Renaissance* (1956) would have enlightened Mr Bell.[13] Scipio Le Squyer was Deputy Chamberlain of the Exchequer, in modern terms Deputy Keeper of the Public Records. Unlike a modern Deputy Keeper, Le Squyer conducted searches for a fee. It was a lucrative job, and in 1632 he was able to move from a tenement in Westminster to a house in Long Acre, and in connection with the move he made a list of his books. It is a subject catalogue of 296 MSS and 487 printed books. Most of the MSS and a lot of the printed books are related to his job, and he has 130 books of divinity, mostly pastoral theology of a puritan tinge. But he has 80 books of what he calls 'Poesy'. This includes

Boccaccio, Chaucer, Spenser, Drayton, *The Ship of Fools*, Du Bartas, Virgil, Ovid and Chapman's Homer. It also includes some plays of Jonson, Kyd, Fletcher and Shakespeare's *Romeo and Juliet* and *Venus and Adonis* – but no *Pericles*. So he must have lent or given away his 1609 quarto some time before 1632. In other words, quarto plays, if unbound, were not treated very seriously – they could be read and discarded.

Le Squyer also has volumes of epigrams: Martial, Harington and two volumes of the plagiarist Henry Parrot. But as well as 'Poesy', Le Squyer has a section of 46 books which he classifies as 'Morality'. This includes Spenser's *Shepherds Calendar*, More's *Utopia*, the Essays of Bacon and Montaigne, and Cicero and Plutarch. So far so good. But 'Morality' also includes the Amsterdam edition (1625) of *Love's School*, the English translation of Ovid's *Ars Amatoria*, and a translation of Synesius on baldness: *A Paradox, proving by reason and example that baldness is much better than bushie hair* (1579). He has some books on the tobacco question and the woman question, including Swetnam's *Araignment of Women* and Dekker's *Batchelars Banquet* (1603), which is a translation of *Les quinze joies de mariage*, a 15th-century French satire. Le Squyer's attitude to the classification 'Morality' was, to say the least, ambiguous, but then some of the books were themselves ambiguous. Le Squyer had a copy of *A Help to Discourse*,[14] an amazingly popular little book which ran to 17 editions between 1618 and 1682. The first edition was called *A help to discourse or a miscellany of merriment*, but by the 6th edition it had become *A help to discourse, or a miscellany of seriousness with merriment* – so that you could classify it under 'Morality'. The contents were equally ambiguous. It begins with a section on Divinity, and what looks like a religious catechism – 'Question: What is the most ancient of all things. Answer: God, because he hath no beginning'. But this soon degenerates into trivialities like 'Question: What number is the most vital among men. Answer: Eight, because 8 souls were only preserved in the Ark, and 8 only mentioned in the scripture to be raised from death to life.' After the catechism comes a series of potted romances: the history of St George, St Christopher and the Seven Sleepers. Then come some epigrams and epitaphs, including an epitaph

> Upon a Chambermaid.
>
> Underneath this stone is laid
> A lady's sometime chambermaid:
> Who was young and plump and pretty
> And yet a maid – alas 'twas pity.

This is followed by riddles and jests, and then by a ready-reckoner and advice for gardeners. *Helps to Discourse* is an excellent example of a very crude form of joco-serious book.

Le Squyer's library catalogue, therefore, reveals a high-ranking civil servant of puritan inclinations, with a distinct taste for light and frivolous reading, which he tries to square with his conscience, and with his subject catalogue.

SIR ROBERT GORDON OF GORDONSTOUN (1580-1656)

Individual items of Sir Robert Gordon's library are well known: he owned many unique and rare STC books, 57 of which are in the Britwell Catalogue and many others are referred to in Lowndes's *Bibliographer's Manual*. But the man and his books have not been considered together.

Sir Robert Gordon was a remarkable man, even if he had never owned a remarkable library.[15] He was the fifth son of Alexander 12th Earl of Sutherland and his second wife Jean, Countess of Sutherland who had been Bothwell's first wife before Bothwell married Mary Queen of Scots. Gordon studied at St Andrews and Edinburgh, and for three years in France, where he visited all the Huguenot strongholds and was greatly influenced by Philippe de Plessis Mornay. On the accession of James I, Gordon came to London and in 1606 was appointed gentleman of the privy chamber and in 1609 was knighted. In 1613 he married the daughter of John Gordon, Dean of Salisbury – her mother was a French Huguenot aristocrat. In 1615 he became 'tutor at law' of his young nephew John 14th Earl of Sutherland, who was a minor: in other words, Gordon was the effective ruler of the County of Sutherland, and he spent much of his time resisting the incursions of the Earl of Caithness. In 1625 he was a go-between in the marriage negotiations of Charles and Henrietta Maria. In the early stages of the Civil War in Scotland he tried to act as a mediator but in 1643 he retired to Gordonstoun. Gordon spent much of his life commuting between the Highlands, London and Salisbury, and he tells us that at one period he rode from Scotland to England six times in 15 months – and for many years he must have travelled up and down at least twice a year.

Sir Robert Gordon's library consists of about 2,000 books and was sold at auction in 1816; apart from the printed auction catalogue there is also a manuscript catalogue in the National Library of Scotland. It is a fascinating collection. He has the church fathers in folio and most of the Calvinist classics; he has ten volumes of William Prynne and nine volumes of Robert Parsons; ten pamphlets of Thomas Scot and all the available prose pamphlets of Milton. He has not much of major historical writings, but he has 23 volumes of quarto political pamphlets relating to the troubles in England and Scotland between 1638 and 1643. But in contrast to that there is a quite remarkable collection of more than 60 French romances, mostly dating from the 1620s and 1630s and mostly published at Rouen. These books seem to be almost standardised productions – black letter quartos with quaint woodcuts – often to be found in other libraries bound in blocks of ten or so at a time. One may be surprised to find that Gordon had a French edition of Tyll Eulenspiegel: *Tiel Ulespiègle, de sa vie, de ses faits et merveilleuses finesses* (Rouen 1625). One thinks of Eulenspiegel as typically Germanic humour, but on looking at the book itself it becomes clear that the French have transformed it into the external form of a romance. Gordon also had English romances, including the source of *Much Ado*, Peter Beverley's verse translation of Ariosto, *The History of Ariodanto and Jenevra* (c.1575: STC 745.5):[16] the only surviving copy is Gordon's copy in the Huntington.

Gordon was also addicted to *facetiae* and *joco-seria*, in Latin, French and English. He has almost all the English books on the woman question, and on hermaphrodites. He has books on smoking and drinking, including Richard Brathwaite's *A Solemn Jovial Disputation briefly shadowing the Law of Drinking* (1617) which is a translation of Blasius Multibibus (pseud.), *Disputatio Inauguralis Theoretico-practica. Ius potandi* (Oenozythopoli 1616 sq.), a Germanic mock-legal disputation.[17] Gordon's library is rich in the minor English miscellaneous writers and versifiers, and what he obviously likes are collections of epigrams and squibs, such as Anthony Copley's *Wits, Fits and Fancies* (1614, STC 5740) and its French equivalents: like William Paget, he has *Les Bigarrures* of Des Accords. Gordon has not got Bacon's *Essays*, but he has got the trivial paradoxical essays of Sir William Cornwallis and John Stephens. He also likes comic dialogues, such as the mock declamation of John Dando and Harry Runt, *Maroccus extaticus, or Banks's Horse in a Trance, in a merry dialogue betwixt Banks and his beast, anatomizing some abuses of the age* (1595, STC 6225), which is referred to in *Love's Labours Lost* and elsewhere: only two copies of *Maroccus extaticus* have survived, and Gordon's is one of them. Again, typically, Gordon has the French equivalent of that sort of thing, the comic declamations attributed to the French actor Tabarin, *Recueil général des rencontres, questions, demandes et autres oeuvres tabariniques*, Arras 1623. Tabarin is another of those minor French burlesque writers that will be found again and again in English private libraries of the 17th century: indeed, one can learn a lot about minor French literature from studying Gordon's catalogue.

Gordon's library is of roughly equal proportions of orthodox calvinist theology, romances, and *facetiae* in English and in French. It is a library clearly reflecting a distinct personality: every book is a personal choice. Gordon was too busy to have much time for serious literature: romances and *facetiae* were for him not really 'time wasting' but true recreation, an essential part of his concept of civility. He was a true bookman because he was a man of action and not at all 'bookish' in the pejorative sense.

EDWARD 2ND VISCOUNT CONWAY (1594-1665)[18]

The library of Edward Conway is mentioned in Lawrence Stone's *Crisis of the Aristocracy* as containing 500 books: in reality it contained 8,000 books, a fact which does not enhance one's opinion of the bibliographical expertise of social historians. A private library of 8,000 books in the middle of the 17th century was remarkable, but Conway was definitely a reader and not a collector and, like Sir Robert Gordon, a man of action: he was a professional soldier and a professional sailor.

He succeeded to his father's title in 1631. Besides the family estate and castle at Lisnegarvey, now Lisburn, Co. Antrim, he had a town house in London and estates at Ragley, Warwickshire. His library was based in Ireland and was looked after by his steward, his chaplain and the local schoolmaster, who had to despatch crates of books to their master wherever he might be, even on the high seas. In 1643 Conway had 4,000 of his books in London which, together with his personal papers, were seized by the Parliament.[19] He bought the books back in 1647, but his papers remained impounded and are now calendared among the State Papers Domestic at the PRO. Conway's portrait is preserved in Clarendon's *History of the Rebellion* like a fly in amber:

He was a voluptuous man in eating and drinking, and of great license in other excesses, and yet was very acceptable to the strictest and gravest men of all conditions. And, which was stranger than all this, he had always from his pleasure, to which his nature excessively inclined him, and from his profession, in which he was diligent enough, reserved so much time for his books and study that he was well versed in all parts of learning, at least appeared like such a one in all occasions and in the best companies.

This is a model of Clarendon's biographical technique – a series of left jabs followed by a right uppercut. But the reading habits of the voluptuous Conway are considerably more interesting than those of the supercilious and dyspeptic Clarendon.

Conway had book buyers in Brussels, Florence and Paris, and in

England he used a variety of booksellers: Philemon Stephens for religious books; Humphrey Moseley for English literature, especially plays; Robert Martin presumably for foreign books; and James Allestree also for foreign as well as English books. When in London, Conway went in person to the Latin warehouse and bought quantities of imported books direct.[20]

Conway's catalogue is a classed catalogue of a very elaborate type, with over 80 separate classifications, and with each classification subdivided into formats. Let us consider it for Conway's light reading. He has 619 plays: 350 English, 241 Italian, 21 Spanish and seven French. The numerical distribution reminds us that in the first half of the 17th century there was not much French drama worth talking about, and Conway has got what there is. But it is the figure of 350 English quarto plays that is the most astonishing. The total output of English printed drama, from the beginning to 1640, was 600 plays. For Conway to have acquired 350 English plays there can be only one explanation: he was buying plays like newsbooks, on a standing order. This is confirmed by a document in the State Papers Domestic printed by Greg. It is a list of plays supplied by Humphrey Moseley to 'an unknown customer'.[21] The customer must have been Conway, as he is the only private individual of this period whose bookbills are in the State Papers, because they were seized in 1643. The plays are supplied in blocks of 10 for five shillings, presumably including binding in boards.

The statistics for Conway's romances are also interesting: out of a total of 343 romances, 128 are French, 79 are Spanish, 72 are Italian, 56 are English, nine are Latin and two are Portuguese. Once again, the numerical distribution reflects availability. As has already been said of Gordon's library, there was almost a mass production of French romances in the 1620s and 1630s. The evidence of Conway's library shows that there was no aristocratic disdain for romances, and no particular linguistic preference. Conway just wanted romances, of whatever language and at whatever literary level – he has even got *Sir Bevis of Hampton*.

The miscellanies, *facetiae*, *joco-seria* etc, are distributed in Conway's catalogue under three headings: *(i) Libri adagiales et eiusmodi*, 55 volumes; *(ii) Scriptores satirici*, 115 volumes; *(iii) Rarae et incertae materiae scriptores*, 59 volumes – a total of 229 volumes. Language distribution is indiscriminately Latin, English, French, Italian and Spanish.

Under *Libri adagiales* Conway has not only Erasmus, but also Arabic and Hebrew proverbs (in Latin), together with Donne's *Juvenilia* (1633), the *Facetie* of Lodovico Domenichi, and Earle's *Microcosmographie* – a curious mixture. Under *Scriptores satirici* he has Petronius, Cornelius Agrippa, Lucian (in French), Lipsius's *Satyra Menippea* (Antwerp 1581), and More's *Utopia*. But he also has the Marprelate tracts, the works of Nashe, and all the literature around Harington's *Metamorphosis of Ajax*. Conway also includes under satire the works of Rabelais – in German as well as in French – and the soft pornography attributed to Pietro Aretino in Italian, French and Spanish: the *Ragionamenti, Le miroir des Courtisans*, Lyon 1580, and *Coloquio de las Damas*, Seville 1607. Also under satire is Donne's *Ignatius his Conclave* (1611) – that work was never considered as serious controversial theology.

The next section, *Rarae et incertae materiae scriptores* includes, to be sure, books on carving, dancing, swimming, acrobatics, falconry, chess, surveying, and how to remove spots and stains from silk. But it also includes 16th-century Italian jestbooks and the miscellanies of Bernardino Baldi. For French there are the *Regrets Facétieux* (Rouen 1632) of Thomassin (i.e.: François d'Amboise), a series of comic epitaphs on dead animals translated from the Italian of Ortensio Landi, and also the comic monologues of Tabarin and Bruscambille, who, like Tabarin, was a French comic actor. The miscellanies in English include *A Banquet of Jests* (1639 STC 1370), only two copies recorded; Robert Chamberlain's *Nocturnal Lucubrations* (1638 STC 4945) and *Conceits, Clinches, Flashes and Whimsies* (1639 STC 4942), only one copy recorded; and purely comic stuff on the woman question like Thomas Heywood's *Curtaine Lecture* (1637 STC 13312) and John Taylor's *Divers Crabtree Lectures* (1639 STC 23747), only one copy recorded. Conway's choice of facetious literature shows that the English material is considerably less sophisticated than the French and Italian.

Two general conclusions can be made about Conway's light reading. First, language is an irrelevance: English has not got a specially favoured position. Secondly, Conway's taste does not exclude lower or middle-class literature: but unlike the peasants and the middle classes, he reads it in all languages.

SIR EDWARD BYSSHE (1615-79)

Bysshe is of course known as a professional herald. A manuscript inventory of his library (of about 2,500 books) values it at £300: the printed auction sale catalogue is dated 15 November 1680.[22] Humfrey Wanley noted that the inventory was 'worthy perusal', and Richard Rawlinson observed that Bysshe's library 'was all well bound and had some very good books in it. The owner a wretch' – Bysshe was a noted toper who turned up on his heraldic visitations so fuddled that he got the genealogies all wrong.

Bysshe's catalogue reveals, as one would expect, the working library of a professional herald, but the reason for referring to it in the present context is because it is the first English auction catalogue to offer, for public sale, a substantial collection of libertine or pornographic books.[23] Bysshe has Aretino's *Ragionamenti* in Italian (three different editions) and in French and Spanish. He also has *La putana errante* (1651), *L'escole des filles* (1667) and Caspar Barthius's *Pornoboscodidascalus* (Francfurt 1624) a Latin translation of the *Celestina*. He has several editions of poésies galantes, chiefly published in the Low Countries in the later 17th century, and also the Paris 1669 edition of that celebrated erotic novel, the *Lettres portugaises* or *Letters of a Portuguese Nun*.[24] Most important of all, perhaps, Bysshe has got that landmark in the history of French libertinage, the anthology of obscene poetry, *Le parnasse des poètes satiriques* (?Paris 1625), usually attributed, wrongly, to the libertine poet Théophile de Viau; only two copies of this, the first edition, have survived: Bib.Nat. and Harvard.[25]

Bysshe's collection of erotica should not be considered in isolation. He has eight volumes of plays and a considerable collection of contemporary English lyric poetry. But more important than that, in the theology section he has over 60 Socinian books published at Rakov.[26] Socinianism, in mid-17th century England, was regarded by the orthodox as something more than half-way to atheism. Bysshe's interest in Socinianism may be part and parcel of his interest in libertinism and in libertine literature. One might even go so far as to say that his reading of erotica was not so much an aberrant symptom of human frailty, but rather a matter of philosophical principle. But even so, whatever the motives, the reading of erotica still remains light reading.

SIR JOSEPH WILLIAMSON (1633-1702)

Sir Joseph Williamson was a self-made man who rose to be Secretary of State by sheer hard work and efficiency: he was not much liked. Pepys referred to him as 'a pretty knowing man and a scholar, but it may be he thinks himself to be too much so' (*Diary*, 6.ii.1663). Williamson had characteristic virtuoso interests: history, genealogy and mathematics. He left his books and manuscripts to Queen's College, Oxford.

Williamson had three library catalogues: an alphabetical catalogue and two subject catalogues.[27] The subject divisions of the first subject catalogue displeased him, and he had the job done again: that is one of the reasons why his library is interesting in the present context. The library consisted of just over 6,000 books. It is rich in travel and trade, and in genealogy and history. His largest section was on law (845 volumes) and he had no less than 236 dictionaries and grammars. Williamson was the second President of the Royal Society, which accounts for 553 books on mathematics and 492 on medicine. He had a number of books on library science (Claudius Clemens,[28] Justus Lipsius, Charles Naudé and Louis Jacob), and the 1674 Bodleian catalogue and many catalogues of foreign booksales and of booksellers. In Williamson's first subject catalogue every kind of literature is put under the heading 'Humanistae'. That did not satisfy Sir Joseph, and he personally went through the whole alphabetical catalogue marking certain items 'P.P.', i.e. 'Poetae', by which he meant fiction as opposed to fact, and including prose as well as poetry. The heading 'Humanistae' was then reserved for 'the classics', which were clearly not reckoned as light reading.

Several features of Williamson's library indicate that it has been formed towards the end of the 17th century. First, the Italian light reading is minimal: he has the Italian classics, Petrarch, Tasso and Ariosto, but he has not got that wealth of minor Italian literature so common in earlier libraries. Secondly, there is none of that unsophisticated popular literature – jest books and wits, fits and fancies – that is to be found in earlier gentry libraries. Thirdly, as far as light reading is concerned, contemporary French literature predominates – over English literature as well as over Italian and Spanish.

Williamson has a number of English plays, but nothing like the sheer quantity of Mostyn, Newdigate or Conway. As for novels, they were all French, or English translations from the French; there were none of the old Spanish romances or their derivatives, and there were no Italian romances. An interesting example of Williamson's French novels is Gabriel Brémond's *Hattige, ou les amours du Roi de Tamarin* (1676), a *roman à clef* on the love affairs of the court of Charles II. Brémond's novels were printed at Amsterdam and published in London by the firm of Magnes and Bentley – they published not only the English translations but also the French originals printed in Holland.

In the field of miscellanies, burlesque and *joco-seria*, Williamson's range was somewhat wider: he had Owen's *Epigrams* and several other collections of epigrams in Latin, Italian and French which occur in the catalogues of an earlier period. For burlesque and satire, Butler's *Hudibras* and some satires on the Rump Parliament are all there is in English: with one or two exceptions, the rest is French. Williamson also has the genuine works of Théophile de Viau, as well as a later edition of the mis-attributed *Parnasse satirique* but, unlike the library of Sir Edward Bysshe, this is not part of a general collection of erotica.

Broadly speaking, then, Williamson did not despise light reading altogether, but it was quite consciously defined, and its range was limited.

The development and decline of the 17th-century private library

Cultural change always comes slowly and erratically, but nevertheless something quite clearly happens to English culture in the course of the 17th century: T.S. Eliot called it 'the dissociation of sensibility'. In terms of the development of the private library, that change is marked by a narrowing of range and interest. First, we no longer find that glorious, haphazard mixture of 'vulgar', or lower-class, literature with 'polite' or upper-class literature. Secondly, as far as modern languages are concerned, we see a multiglot culture narrowing down to a duoglot culture: English and French. What are the factors contributing to this change? In his unpublished Sandars Lectures Professor D.F. McKenzie[29] has already suggested that playbooks are driven out by newsbooks. Three other symptoms may also be considered: (i) the rise of library science; (ii) the rise of critical journalism; (iii) the changed location and status of the library in the private house.

(i)   LIBRARY SCIENCE

The rot set in with John Evelyn who translated Charles Naudé's *Instructions concerning Erecting of a Library* (1661): Pepys wisely commented that Naudé was 'above my reach' (*Diary*, 5.x. 1661). Evelyn's own library, in contrast to Pepys's, is a monumentally dull collection with no light reading at all. Evelyn acquires the sort of books that he thinks a learned man ought to possess, and he wastes his time arranging and re-arranging them, and altering his pressmarks, in order to conform to various systems. With Evelyn the library becomes a monstrous piece of domestic furniture and a prop to bourgeois vanity. Sir Joseph Williamson, by nature a man of system, had, as we have seen, several books of library science, though Williamson was not a conformist in the way that Evelyn was. The 18th century saw the publication of a number of books on how to form a library and the cult of 'the most approved authors', and by the early 19th century we have Dibdin's *Library Companion* (1824), the complete snob's handbook.

(ii)   THE RISE OF CRITICAL JOURNALISM

Critical journalism begins with the *Journal des Savants*, 1665: there was an English imitation in 1683, *Weekly Memorials for the Ingenious*, and by the end of the century Peter Motteux, John Dunton and Samuel Parker ran similar journals. The early 18th century is full of them, and the *Gentleman's Magazine*, founded in 1731 by Edward Cave, turned out to be the most durable.[30] The sequence of Cave's career is significant: newsletter writer, printer, literary editor. In the 18th century it is the book trade that is telling the gentleman, or would-be gentleman, what to read. After the 17th century you do not need to study library catalogues to learn about reading habits –

that can be done by studying the reviews. Private library catalogues, from the 18th century onwards, are primarily only a guide to collecting habits.

(iii) THE CHANGED LOCATION AND STATUS OF THE LIBRARY

The growth of the social status of the private library is a symptom of its cultural decline. At the beginning of the 17th century the gentleman's library was housed in the private part of the house – it was on a level of prestige with the butler's pantry, the gun room or the tack room. By the end of the 17th century the library had become one of the public rooms, an additional sitting room or even a salon.[31] The gentleman's library shelves were thus exposed to the inquisitive gaze of his guests: he now has to show that he has got all the right books, that is to say all the fashionable books, whether or not he has actually read them, or wants to read them.

In other words, the 17th-century gentleman's library, as revealed in his library catalogues, was the last truly 'private' library, revealing real personal reading tastes and habits, uninfluenced by bourgeois conceptions of 'decorum', and uninfluenced by library science, booksellers' puffs, literary critics, or domestic architects.

References

1. W.O. Hassall (ed.) *A Catalogue of the Library of Sir Edward Coke*, London 1950, p.66.
2. For Mostyn and Newdigate see S. de Ricci, *English Collectors*, Cambridge 1930, pp.180-81, 188-9; for Harington and Oxinden see W.W. Greg, *Bibliography of English Printed Drama*, London 1957, III 1306 sq.
3. Bodley Facs. c.22.
4. In 1656 Rogers and Ley published *An Alphabetical Catalogue of all such plays that ever were printed* (Greg, *op.cit.*, 1320 sq.). De Ricci was so struck by the fact that this list corresponded very closely to the plays actually in the Mostyn library that he conjectured that Rogers and Ley must somehow have obtained access to the Mostyn library. A less fanciful explanation is that the Mostyn collection simply contained almost every play known to the trade (see S. de Ricci's preface to H. Medwall, *Fulgens and Lucres*. NY 1920).
5. L.B. Wright, 'The Reading of Plays during the Puritan Revolution', *Huntington Library Bulletin*, 6 (1934), pp.73-108, is useful on this point.
6. Gerard Langbaine's *Momus Triumphans: or the plagiaries of the English Stage expos'd*, London 1688, is symptomatic of the changed circumstances by the end of the century – half a century earlier a gentleman would not need to be told: he possessed the continental originals as well as the English derivatives.
7. Henry Thomas, *Spanish and Portuguese Romances of Chivalry*, Cambridge 1920, p.288.
8. NCBEL I (1974), 2021-43.

9. A good example is William Burton, *Utile Dulce, or Truth's Libertie. Seven Wittie-wise Dialogues, full of delight and fitte for use; verie applicable for these times, but seasonable for all ages*, London 1606 (black letter). It is in fact a selection of anticlerical essays from Erasmus's *Colloquia*.

10. Dr F.W. Van Heertum's introduction to her edition of J. Swetnam's *Araignment of...Women (1615)*, Nymegen 1989, gives a very full documentation of the ambiguity of this genre.

11. P. Elmer (ed.) *The Library of Dr John Webster*, London, 1986, and review in *The Library*, March, 1989, p.72.

12. A very similar book is the *Poematum liber*, London 1573, by the ex-Jesuit Richard Wills: its significance is discussed by J.W. Binns, *Intellectual Culture in Elizabethan and Jacobean England*, Leeds 1990, pp.50 sq. But besides being in Latin, Wills's book only ran to a single edition, though many copies have survived: *Les Bigarrures* was a far more popular vernacular version of the same sort of thing, which was frequently reprinted well into the 17th century.

13. F. Taylor, 'The Books and Manuscripts of Scipio Le Squyer', *Bulletin of the John Rylands Library*, 25 (1941), 137 sq.

14. By W.B., sometimes attributed to William Basse.

15. There is a good article on Gordon in *DNB* and a very perceptive study in David Mathew, *Scotland Under Charles I*, London 1955, pp.169-79. Gordon's *Genealogical History of the Earldom of Sutherland*, Edinburgh 1813, is partly an autobiography. BL 1508/1274 is the auction catalogue with buyers and prices.

16. C.T. Prouty, *The Sources of Much Ado about Nothing*, New Haven 1951.

17. For some English locations of the Latin editions of Blasius Multibibus see the old STC 3557-61. They have been eliminated from the new STC.

18. Conway's catalogue, and a few of his books, are in the Public Library, Armagh. My former research student, Margret de Wit, is preparing a full study of Conway and his books, and I am most grateful to her for the loan of a microfilm of the catalogue.

19. See the article by I. Roy, 'The library of Edward, 2nd Viscount Conway', *Bulletin of the Institute of Historical Research*, May 1968, pp.35-46.

20. H.R. Plomer, 'A Cavalier's Library', *The Library*, 2nd series, Vol.5, 1904, pp.158-172; David Mathew, *The Social Structure in Caroline England*, Oxford 1948, also makes use of the Conway papers in the PRO.

21. Greg, *op. cit.*, pp.1317-18.

22. W.H. Godfrey and A. Wagner, *The College of Arms*, London 1963, p.53; B.L. MS Harl. 813 ff.174-99. The inventory belonged to Bp. Stillingfleet, who also acquired a number of books from Bysshe's library. A marked copy of the auction catalogue is at ULC Syn. 5.67.2: I am grateful to David McKitterick for this information.

23. For an introduction to this sort of literature, see D.F. Foxon, *Libertine Literature in England 1660-1745*, NY 1965.

24. Sometimes attributed to Marianna d'Alcoforado.

25. Roméo Arbour, *L'ère baroque en France 1616-28*, Genève 1979, II 1975.

26. Bysshe's Socinianism is discussed in H.J. McLachlan, *Socinianism in 17th century England*, Oxford 1951.

27. I am most grateful to Miss Helen Powell, of Queen's College Library, for drawing my attention to Williamson's catalogues.

28. Claudius Clemens, *Musaei, sive Bibliothecae tam privatae quam publicae extructio, instructio, cura, usus*, Lugd. 1635, was very influential in its day, though not perhaps

sufficiently well known to modern historians of library science. Clemens deplores the reading of romances and of trivia but, sensible Jesuit that he is, he accepts it as a fact of life.

29. D.F. McKenzie, *The London Booktrade in the later 17th century*, 1970, p.73; typescript at B.L. Ac.2660.m.(28).
30. There is a full bibliography in NCBEL II 1291-1312.
31. M. Girouard, *Life in the English Country House*, Harmondsworth 1980, pp.166-179. When Thomas Pennant visited Mostyn Hall at the end of the 18th century he reported: 'at one end of this building is the library, a room most unworthy of the valuable collection of manuscripts and books it contains' – in other words the library was still where it had been at the beginning of the 17th century (see T. Pennant, *History of the parishes of Whiteford and Holywell*, London 1796).

William Herbert: his library and his friends

ROBIN MYERS

'Similar propensities and endowments soon discover one another,' wrote William Beloe, 'and induce frequent and familiar associations. Generally speaking, in London, at least, there is great liberality among literary men, a ready disposition to interchange communications, which may be mutually useful, to accommodate one another with the loan of books, to point out sources of information, indeed to carry on, by a sort of common treaty among one another, a pleasant, friendly, and profitable commerce.[1]

THUS WILLIAM HERBERT (1718-1795) in accumulating his very large library, which he made use of in revising and enlarging Joseph Ames's original edition of the *Typographical Antiquities*, 1749, learnt to mix business with pleasure, commerce with social intercourse, book, print and map selling with book-collecting, and publishing with bibliography and authorship.

William Herbert (1718-1795) and his friends

The family may have been a cadet branch of the Herberts of Pembrokeshire, since William used the family Wyvern crest on the covers of a few of his books, and a bookplate (of which more below) with the Herbert armorial bearings. He was the third generation of a family of dyers and members of the Drapers' Company, the second of five children of Thomas Herbert, the younger, draper and stocking presser of Gravel Lane, Southwark. According to the unreliable Dibdin[2] he went to school in Hitchin, was bound to a hosier and his 'career commenced in the service of the East India Company as purser's clerk to three of their ships'. '?Poss went to India before 1748' is pencilled against his entry in the registers at Drapers' Hall. In the age of mercantile expansion a city youth might take the opportunity of seeing the world by trading overseas, in the way a young nobleman went on the grand tour. After a series of misadventures in India, Herbert returned to London by 1745,[3] and was made free of the Drapers' Company in 1748. Dibdin avers, on what grounds I know not, that he made the transition from dyeing to printselling by turning to painting on glass. The switch in his trade is less improbable when we learn that there was an established tradition of print-selling in the Drapers' Company[4] and bear in mind that he had been drawing charts while in the employ of the East India Company. He took a 14-year lease on 'one of ten houses lately built on the north-east part of London Bridge', where, according to the index of the Bridge House Rentals and Accounts[5] he set up as a print-seller and bound two apprentices who both subsequently set up as print-sellers.[6] When the bridge caught fire, in 1758, he took advantage of the topicality to publish a history of the bridge with the imprint *'sold by William Herbert on the remains of London Bridge, with an engraving of the temporary bridge after the fire,* (1s. plain, 1s.6d. coloured)'.[7] The next year, 1759, as the bridge houses began to be pulled down, he moved to 27 Goulston Square, Whitechapel, and began to develop the publishing side of his business, issuing frequent lists, according to Dibdin (p.77) of 'Books, Charts,and Maps Printed for William Herbert'. He had commenced his authorial-editorial career with *A new directory of the East-Indies with general and particular charts for the navigation of those seas...* 1758, and finding that it sold, he published a second edition, 1759, 'with additions, corrections, and explanatory notes...printed for the editor'. Over the imprint 'printed for W. Herbert by T. Spilsbury', he published the first edition of Nichelson's *Sundry Remarks and Observations made in a Voyage to the East Indies...* 1758, then combined the two publications, and issued in all 5 editions between 1759 and 1780.[8] He started on his writing career in earnest by interleaving and annotating a copy of the 1765 edition.[9] The publishing and auto-publishing pattern thus established, he bought the plates and remaining stock of Atkyns's *History of Glocestershire*, originally published in 1712, but according to Gough 'rendered extremely scarce from the number of copies that were burnt' in the fire which destroyed the printing-office of William Bowyer (1712).[10] Herbert's edition was, perhaps, a slow seller as copies appeared in Arrowsmith and Bowley's auction of Herbert books in 1798; lot 191 was a copy with 73 plates.

According to Dibdin, Herbert married three times. We know nothing of his first wife. It would seem that his second was a niece of Thomas Newman[(*)], a dissenting minister and son of a linen draper. Dibdin describes her, on what authority I cannot say, as a woman of means but of weak intellect. His third wife, Phillippa Croshold, was a niece of Robert Masham (1707-97)[(*)] of Stratton Strawless, in Norfolk – to whom he left a mourning ring in his will – an antiquary, through whom, perhaps, Herbert came into

---

[(*)]Signifies a name that appears in the Biographical Index (see pp.154-155).

the circle of Norfolk antiquaries who included Sir John Fenn (1739-1794)[*]. In a letter to Fenn, 1751, he writes of 'visiting my wife's Uncle, Mr M. of Stratton Strawless'. Thomas Martin assisted Herbert and corresponded with him. (See D. Stoker, p.101 above.) Herbert had no children, though much married, at least none acknowledged. There is, however, a rumour that his nephew, Isaac Herbert[*], print- and bookseller was, in reality, his son; a manuscript note on one Bodleian copy of Postan's auction catalogue of April 2nd 1798 refers to Herbert's 'nephew, son (?) Isaac...Clerk to Arrowsmith the auctioneer & ci-devant Book Jobber'. It is the only suggestion of sexual indiscretion.

Herbert continued to be active in the Drapers' Company all his life, moving steadily through the ranks to become Master Warden in 1792.[11] He was punctilious in attending Courts; he attended his last Court on 22 January 1795, and died six weeks later, 15 March. About 1773, he 'purchased a country residence at Cheshunt which he enlarged and adorned in a style of some taste; so as to make it one of the most respectable villas in the neighbourhood' (Dibdin p.78) but he continued trading until 1776 when he sold his chart- and print-selling business to Henry Gregory, allegedly for £1,000, being then 58 years old.[12] He seems never to have retired completely, continuing to publish or reissue his publications as well as dealing in books, sometimes helping his nephew in his book- and print-selling business.

But he was now free to enjoy the life of the gentleman scholar and give most of his energy to book collecting and to the revision of Ames's *Antiquities*, which occupied him for the rest of his life. In these retirement years he travelled to Norfolk from time to time, and to London regularly, probably timing his visits to coincide with the Draper's Courts, although Dibdin says nothing of that reason: 'When occupied with taking extracts from the Caxtonian volumes in his Majesty's library, his usual custom was to come to town for a week or ten days during moonlight nights to his friends Mr and Mrs Dennis, in Cowper's Row, Crutched Friars...' (Dibdin p.88). He also received visits from antiquarians passing through Cheshunt on their way to London. William White[*] wrote 24 April 1774 of 'the pleasure of being with you...at Cheshunt'.[13]

The picture emerges of a thriving 18th-century City man whose livery company connections, early employment in the East India Company, print and map dealing, topographical and hydrographical publishing, brought him into contact with gentleman collectors and the more cultured members of the book trade. It was a world at once cosy and diverse. Lockyer Davis[*], the learned bookseller and Master of the Stationers' Company, introduced him into Stationers' Hall where he was allowed to borrow and copy the early registers, and he saw (perhaps dining in the Hall) a list, long since vanished, of benefactors of the Company. His relations with Alexander Dalrymple (1737-1808)[*], Hydrographer to the Admiralty, former servant of the East India Company and book collector on a vast scale, exemplifies the way that friendship grew from a business association because there was a common interest in acquiring books and, in Herbert's case, selling those he did not want. We can chart the development of their friendship through their correspondence.[14] In May 1772 Dalrymple wrote formally in the third person to ask if he might make use of certain charts which Herbert had drawn of the South China Seas. The correspondence continued on the same subject, from January 1774 in the first person until April 1779, when Dalrymple wrote in a cordial tone:

The East India Company have set me to work, as you will perceive by the inclosed...as all my Collection of Charts are still in India, I will esteem it a favour if you will be so obliging to let me copy ['a draught of the Strait of Lombock'] over again. I think you also mentioned having many views in the Strait of Malacca, and various Journals in different parts of India, if you should be inclined to part with them, I will be obliged to you to let me know what they are, and what value you put upon them.

By now they were on visiting terms and in June Dalrymple, after postponing a visit to Cheshunt owing to 'an unlucky accident', wrote from Soho Square, 30 June 1779: 'I intend to do myself the pleasure to make you a visit on Saturday next if I do not hear of your being engaged. I cannot do more than make you a visit and return in the evening.' In December he was drawing Herbert's attention to a 'Catalogue of Books now on sale by Thomas King'[*] in which 'I perceive there are many English books before 1600. I thought this intimation might be satisfactory to you...'. The book talk fanned out into discussion of George Wither and emblem books, which were among Dalrymple's collecting interests, and to lending or exchanging books from their respective libraries. By February 1785 Dalrymple had asked Sir Joseph Banks[*] to let Herbert 'have the inspection of the Museum Catalogue, so far as already printed, and he in the most obliging manner said that he would put it into your possession for any reasonable time if you would call on him. Whenever you come to town I will accompany you to his house.' In the same letter Dalrymple has 'picked out a few old books for your inspection. If you have done with my book that contains the copies of different types, I beg you to bring it with you.'

Herbert's book-collecting and the *Typographical Antiquities*

The *Typographical Antiquities* (1749) was the first serious account of English printing and printers to 1600, based on the material which its author Joseph Ames (1689-1759)[*] had spent years in collecting for his own interest. He had not intended to publish but was persuaded to do so when Samuel Palmer's long-awaited *General History of England* (1732), hastily completed after his death by George Psalmanazar, failed, according to John Nichols,[15] to 'answer the expectations of the Publick'. Although Ames and Herbert inhabited the same small world of the City, the two men never met (Ames was 55 when Herbert returned from the East), nor did Herbert ever become a Fellow of the Society of Antiquaries of which Ames was secretary and to which so many of his friends belonged. Ames's library was auctioned by Langford (5 May 1760) the year after his death.[16] Sir Peter Thompson (1698-1770)[*], merchant, collector and Ames's long-standing friend, bought heavily, and it seems that a good deal was for resale. He sold to Herbert as is well-known, Ames's copy of the *Typographical Antiquities*, interleaved and annotated 'with 100 articles in manuscript' (lot 1298) and 'the copper plates, blocks and copyright of the same Book' (lot 1299) for nine guineas. On the face of it a comparison of the library of the instigator of the *Antiquities*, as we might call Ames, with that of its 'continuator' as De Ricci dubbed Herbert (*English Collectors of Books*, p.58), should reveal a good deal about the changing taste and technique of collecting in the intervening half century as well of the temperament and working methods of the two men: but, despite Ames's ownership notes in the *Antiquities*, which amplify our knowledge of his English books before 1600, it is not easy to get the feel of what seems to have been a fairly typical, medium-sized, mid-18th century collection, now completely dispersed. We know that Ames must have disposed of some of his Caxtons in his lifetime[17] but we cannot trace his books in the way we can do with Herbert's larger, better documented collection.

The purchase of the *Antiquities* revolutionised Herbert's book collecting and publishing life. From then until the end of his life the revision of Ames and book collecting were twin activities. Using *Ames* as a guide he set to work to fill the gaps in his black-letter collection and 20 years later, having 'thought there could not be offered a more acceptable present to the lovers of science than a republication of this work with the author's own improvements, and what further could be collected from my own observations, and those of my learned friends', he 'in 1780 circulated proposals for printing the work by subscription in two volumes...' (Preface vi).

On the verso of a marbled wrapper bound into the front of Ames's interleaved copy he listed the initials of the owners of books whose provenance he gives in the *Antiquities*, together with a 'list of marks used by gentlemen' (the first generation of Norfolk antiquaries, I learn from David Stoker) 'when they had look'd over writings or books'. His forthcoming book opened many library doors and made him the centre of the bibliographical and bibliophilic coterie into which he had been steadily moving since 1760. As he said, 'in the mean time my printed proposals proved a powerful inducement with gentlemen who had any materials proper for this work to communicate them...'. This proved very useful when it came to bidding at their posthumous sales and:

In the several libraries of James West, John Ratcliffe, and William Bayntun, esqrs. the Rev. Mr Cole of Milton, the Rev. Dr Giffard, of the British Museum, Sir John Hawkins, knight, Dr Ducarel[(*)], Mr Tutet...i[18] had free access during the lives of their owners; and since their decease many articles have been transferred into my own library. i forbear to insist on a collection which has employed no inconsiderable part of my life and, i may add, my fortune in forming it as the reader will find so frequent reference to it.

Two of Ames's notable books reached Herbert's collection by just such a circuitous route: lot 1089, 'the Nychodemus Gospel, emprynted by Wynkyn de Worde 1532' with 'the Most excellent Treatise of the thre Kynges of Coleyne imperfect' (I believe this to be the 1526 edition, though no date is given in the catalogue). It was lot 770 in the sale of John Ratcliffe's library (1776) when Herbert bought it for 5*s*.6*d*. and put his book plate in it. Wynkyn de Worde's *Thre Kynges of Coleyne* (1526), sold by Sothebys in the Phillipps sale of 1973, was catalogued with the note: 'Previously owned by William Herbert, bibliographer, with his signature on the fly leaf and a book plate of a later member of the Herbert family'. Traylen used the same note in his catalogue no.90 (1980) and priced the book at £2,200. Andrew Sokol recently sold it to a North American library.[19]

The Baker-Bagford-Harleian *Canterbury Tales I*, was catalogued as 'although imperfect...suppos'd to be the most perfect in the Kingdom' (lot 821 in Ames's sale). Sir Peter Thompson bought it and it reappeared at Mark Cephas Tutet's[(*)] sale, 15 February 1786, where Herbert paid a guinea (lot 362) for it. The surviving correspondence shews Herbert mixing business with pleasure, hunting for books for friends who were also customers, or fellow dealers, borrowing books, and, after 1774, offering hospitality at Cheshunt as well as receiving information from, or introductions to, other learned gentlemen. George Mason[*] was one from whom he 'received many curious articles'. Mason hoped (Feb. 1779) 'by the middle of next week to bring [a parcel of books] to town with him, and will lodge them at Mr White's where Mr Herbert will have an opportunity of looking it over. Mr Mason intends putting a scrap of paper in each book, with the reason of bringing it. Where Mr Herbert sees no paper, he may conclude the books totally omitted by Ames'.[20]

Subscribers eagerly awaited the work announced for publication in 1780 and almost every correspondent thereafter refers to it, sometimes with thinly veiled impatience. Sir John Fenn in Dereham 5 February 1781, was 'pleased to hear that the delay of your work did not proceed from want of health but as the delay adds to its perfection I will wait with patience'.

William White, writing on June 9 1783, was another who, 'shall think it no small pleasure if you can spare the time soon to here [*sic*] from you and how the above work goes on'. White kept up a steady correspondence with Herbert on personal as well as book subjects after he moved to Crickhowell, near Abergavenny, though he kept a London base. Bibliographers never mention him, though he was clearly a serious, if personally a somewhat tedious, collector. He had good and literate things to say about his books but wrote them in an illiterate hand. Herbert seems at times to act as his agent or scout for he writes, 3 July 1780:

the books you have found by you, some of 'em I missed when I came to pack up my books. As to the first three named, hold 'em for me till another time and the three next, viz Ames, *Destruction of Troy*, *Glass of Government*, *English Roman Life*, Please to keep if you think them worth the three first. The rest of them that is with you, if you have the least desire for them please take them at your estimation which I am sure will be satisfactory to me and account for 'em when I pay you for that desired work of yours Tipographical Antiquities ...'.

He ends with cordial greetings of June 9 1783, 'Mrs White joines [*sic*] in best respects to Mrs Herbert and self and to Master Izack...'

Richard Farmer[*], Master of Emmanuel College, Cambridge, 'who from his earliest years has availed himself of opportunities that have fallen to the lot of few collectors...' (Preface viii) gave Herbert 'free access' to his large collection. he also opened doors usually closed to a non-university man, and arranged for Herbert to work with Bishop More's books at the University Library, Edward Capel's at Trinity College and the Pepysian library at Magdalene.

William Cole[*], who lived at Milton, Cambs., borrowed two volumes of 'scarce Tracts by Wynkyn de Worde' which included the Nychodemus Gospell from the University Library, Cambridge in December 1781 and examined them for Herbert. The first volume, as he told Herbert, contained 'no less than 26 tracts, full of wooden cuts'. He was very ill, as he wrote to Richard Gough[*], 16 December 1781, being 'very bad in the night with flying gout about my stomache', but 'I must *hurry to Mr Herbert's wants*...I have finished Mr Herbert's request in 46 pages, in the very midst of indisposition & am so ill I can hardly hold my pen.' Indeed, his letter to Herbert is written in a hand so shaky as to be barely decipherable: 'The two volumes came to hand only last night, and must be returned to the University Library by Friday morning...Had I been well and more Time allowed, I might have looked into each Tract more minutely, as it is you must excuse my perfunctory performance & believe me, sir, I am a hearty well wisher to your laudable studies...'. In Nichols's printed version of this letter, Cole added, 'I knew Mr Ames personally, corresponded with him, and have been many times at his house at Wapping, to see his prints, and purchase some of them...'. He did not live to see Herbert's *Ames* published; he died exactly a year later.[21]

Frederic Barnard, the King's librarian, was unfailingly helpful, as was John Price (1734-1813), for 45 years Bodley's librarian, who corresponded at some length with Herbert, and gave him an introduction to the Dowager Duchess of Portland, Edward Harley, Earl of Oxford's widow, who, 'most obligingly brought her scarce "Noble Boke of Festes"' (the *Book of Cookery*, Pynson, 1500) 'to town for my inspection and very condescendingly told me, if i would come to Bulstrode, when she was there, she would allow me the use of her library; but it pleased God to take her before that opportunity offered.' (Preface viii).

And for Scotland, that dubious antiquary, John Pinkerton, (1758-1826)[*] then staying in Kentish Town, lent a new acquisition, which Herbert sent his nephew to collect for him: 'My nephew, who brings you this, will take great care of it, and convey it safe to me; and as i purpose being in London the latter end of this month, or the beginning of the next, will then wait on you with it...'[22]

Herbert's early collecting: book-plate evidence
'If we may judge from his first occupations in life,' wrote Dibdin, 'a love of books does not seem to have been a favourite passion of his youth' (p.74). It has always been assumed that Herbert's book-collecting dated from the start of his work on the revision of Ames, but a single dated (1745) example

Herbert's book-plate

of Herbert's anonymous, armorial bookplate proves that he must have considered himself a collector by the time he was 27,[23] some 15 years before his purchase of Ames's interleaved volume turned him to the avid pursuit of early books. He is in the long-established tradition of collectors who commission a book-plate in a fit of enthusiasm and then find it too much of a chore to stick it into their books. I have tracked down only seven books bearing the book-plate, as well as three with the Herbert wyvern crest impressed on the top cover,[24] and it is not to be wondered at that librarians and bibliographers have paid no attention to this particular anonymous mark of ownership. 'Every volume bore on the title-page his signature' and 'there is hardly an English collection in which some specimens of his library are not to be found,' De Ricci stated categorically. He was writing of the early books, all bought in the second half of his life when he was at work on the *Antiquities*. A man who possessed a book-plate he did not use probably owned books he did not sign, but it is making bricks without straw to attempt to reconstruct the young Herbert's collection from a single dated *ex-libris* not attached to a book. Even for that portion of his library which is well documented it would be a herculean task to do for Herbert's collection what Professor Corsten has so admirably done for Thomas Baker's.[25] Still, we will indulge in a little idle speculation all the same. May not some of his books on hydrography and oriental travel date from his earliest years? They would have been useful when he returned from service with the East India Company, and set up as a printseller and engraver of charts. Herbert may also have been combining business with pleasure when he acquired the copyright in Nichelson's *Sundry Remarks...in a voyage to the East Indies*. Map and chart publishing may have led him to topography and to the purchase and reissue of Atkyn's *History of Glocestershire* since he interleaved and annotated a copy of it. He does not seem to have made London books a speciality, either as publisher (except for the London Bridge work) or collector, though he owned such standard works as Stow, and Pennant. Yet London would seem an obvious choice for a City and Gilds man trading in prints and topography and collecting materials on early English printing history, so much London-centred.

The range of his collection
Scrutiny of Herbert's purchases at sales shews that he was far more catholic in his book-buying than has hitherto been thought. In addition to his early books, which included some 24 Caxtons, 38 or so Wynkyn de Wordes, and 45 Pynsons, he filled his shelves, as other gentlemen did, with law, the classics in the original and in translation, French and Italian books, dictionaries and grammars, 'antiquities' and history, some genealogy, natural history, medicine, a certain amount of standard English literature and much else. Not only has it hitherto been assumed that Herbert's book-collecting was wholly directed towards his revision of the *Antiquities* but also that he was not interested in the contents of his books; his marginalia and working papers all concern provenance and bibliographical details connected with his great work but the fact is that reading for pleasure is not usually done with the pen poised for annotation. Then again, the surviving correspondence dates from the last decades of his life when he was increasingly preoccupied with his revision of the *Antiquities*, as he fell farther and farther behind his publication deadline.

Interest in the subject may have occasioned such purchases as *News from the Sea...* 1609, (West's sale, 1773) Goughe's *Original of the Turkish Empire*, 1561, (Ratcliffe's sale, 1776), and *Drake's Voyages into the East Indies*, 1681, (lot 126) and in the Arrowsmith and Bowley sale, such contemporary travel books as Carver's *Travels in North America*, 1779 (lot 105), Coxe, *Voyages en Pologne, Russie, Suede, Danemarc*, 3 vols. 1786 (lot 180), and Beaumont's *Travels through the Maritime Alps*, 1795 (lot 200).

18th-century gentlemen may not have read in foreign languages as fluently as their 17th-century forebears (see T. Birrell, above, p.124) but it would be nice to think that Herbert's travels stimulated interest in foreign languages and that Stephen's *Spanish Grammar*, 1739 (lot 661 in the Arrowsmith and Bowley sale), Altieri's *Italian Method of Learning the Greek Tongue*, 1749 (lot 19), Grose's *Classical Dictionary of the Vulgar Tongue*, 1788 (lot 237), and Richards's *Welsh and English Dictionary*, Bristol 1753 (lot 534), and the Italian, Spanish and Bengali dictionaries in Isaac Herbert's 1796 catalogue were Herbert's private books, acquired for use. Unfortunately we have not the bookseller's assurance, as we have with the sale of John Hutton's[*] library, sold 1764,[26] that 'Not a single lot in this collection, but what was the property of the Deceased'. Indeed we are specifically told that these are mixed sales, with book-sellers' stock and other unnamed properties included with books from Herbert's library, and so much must remain speculation – though he may also have acquired a good many books by accident, as it were, in mixed lots,[27] and surely one curious volume of Alphabets in *Sanscret, Telenga, Malabar, Singhali, Chinese, Tartar, Syamese ...and exercises of the languages etc. 18 copper plates & a map of the country*, 7s.6d. was Herbert's own.

'In regard to his moral and religious character, Herbert was correct and devout. In principles, he was a strict Presbyterian, but had the good sense never to exact a conformity of opinion, on religious subjects, from those who were more closely united with him.' (Dibdin p.89.) Interest in theology must have been a motive for buying such a profusion of 'divinity' and religious tracts of all shades of belief from dissenting to Roman Catholic. He may have collected Bibles from mixed motives of piety and bibliophily; 'Mr Herbert contributed' to Ames's original list of English bibles (1526-1757), 'not a few articles from his own collection', observed Nichols[28] but Herbert's collection also numbered bibles in both modern and classical languages – the Arrowsmith & Bowley sale contained '*La Sainte Bible*, 2 vol. Elzevir 1669' (lot 206), the '*Bible Latina, cum Concord.* with wood cuts, 1516' (lot 207) and a recent Hebrew Bible, the *Biblia Hebraica Kennicotti*, 2 vols, Oxford 1776 (lot 205).

Herbert bought manuscripts as well as books, and these had little bearing on his revision of the *Antiquities*. The Arrowsmith and Bowley sale contained 94 lots of manuscripts, among them a 'breviarum with the music in score, on vellum', (lot 874), five illuminated missals, lots 880, 892, 903, 956, 959, two books of hours (lots 844 and 892), manuscript bibles, medical manuscripts and a variety of historical documents, such as a vellum manuscript 'relative to the marriage of Henry VIII and Anne Cleves' which he bought at West's sale of curiosities for 11s., (lot 64), and 'Orders for his

Highness Court given at Richmond 1610 being the orders for Prince Henry's household *c..*1621-30' which he later sold to Francis Douce.[29] He had several genealogical manuscripts, such as that of the Progenitors and Visitation of Norfolk, 'with the descents of the chiefest houses...1563', £2.2*s.*, lot 64 in Isaac Herbert's sale.

Business combined with pleasure
By the mid-1760s Herbert had become a frequenter of the sale rooms and was skilled in the technique of buying at the right price. At the posthumous sale of John Hutton, 1764, he bought 181 mostly large mixed lots, probably for stock or resale. It is most notable that he did not bid on the first day's lots of library catalogues and bibliographical works which he would have snapped up a few years later.

He seems, on occasion, to have acted on behalf of customers, or friends. He acted for John Ratcliffe[(*)] and William White at the Leigh and Sotheby sale of British Museum duplicates, 4 April 1769 and wrote to Ratcliffe, 5 April, to tell him how he had fared:

I just got time enough today to Mr Baker's to buy lot 231 for you, it cost 3/9. I brought it home with me, and will bring it with me next Saturday se'night. I am very sorry I was not time enough for the other lot for your friend White, but don't know whether I should have ventured to hve purchased it, as it went for £25.6*s...*'[30]

Herbert's purchases at auction
By the early 1770s 'our Antiquary' was prosperous enough 'to live in a style of comfort and ease... and gratify his passion for literature and antiquities. He attended book sales, and made frequent purchases...his application to possess himself of every article or information, that libraries or auctions could furnish him with, was intense.' (Dibdin p.77.) James West[(*)] was among those whose 'several libraries' Herbert 'had free access' to 'during the lives of their owners' and from whose posthumous sales he was able to 'transfer many articles' to his own library. West's enormous collections were sold by Langford in three sales (1773) – Curiosities and MSS, 19 January; Prints and Books of prints, 3 February; and a 24-day sale of books (4,653 lots, totalling £2,910) on 29 March.[31] Herbert was a major buyer and his purchases in the book sale are a good guide to the eclecticism of his taste. There were few sections where he abstained from bidding and among the hundreds of lots which he bought were quantities of religious tracts, mostly in mixed lots costing only shillings, bibles of various dates, classical texts and the classics in translation, and most of the other classes of book

mentioned above. He also bought Caxtons including the *Lyf of our Lady*, lot 1862, for £2.12*s*, *Golden Legend*, lot 1865, £12.15*s*., the *Cordiale*, 1480, lot 1873, for the high price of £14, and a number of Wynkyn de Wordes and other black-letter volumes mostly ranging in price from 2 guineas to £5. In the Curiosities sale Wyclif's *Testament*, lot 76, 'wrote about the time of Henry VI in the year 1425', cost him £4.7*s*.

Ratcliffe was one of his main rivals at the West sale but he got a second chance to buy some of the lots he had lost when Ratcliffe's library came under the hammer three years later.[32] Among the 50 or more lots of early theological works, bibles and the like which he bought were Calvin's sermons, 1577, lot 99. 3*s*., Littleton's *Tenures*, Tottel, 1581, 'and 5 more', lot 525, 2*s*.,6*d*., Caxton's Mirk. *Liber Festivalis*, 1483, lot 1020, £3, and Caxton's *Canterbury Tales II* '...made perfect by MSS', lot 1021, £4 (later the Spencer-Rylands copy), as well as Goughe's *Turkish Empire*, 1561, lot 509, 2*s*.6*d*., Wynkyn de Worde *Nychodemus Gospel*, 1532, and *Three Kynges of Coleyne* [1526], lot 770, 8*s*.6*d*., already mentioned.

At the sale[33] of Mark Cephas Tutet's 'small but valuable library', 15 February 1786, Herbert bought eight choice lots. He bought three early books – Ames's *Canterbury Tales I* (already discussed) 'imperfect, £1.1*s*.', lot 362, '*A Primer into English for the Use of Children, after the Use of Sarum*...no date', lot 163, 12*s*., and '*The Lyfe of St. Francis*, printed by Pynson, sine anno', lot 319, 14*s*.6*d*. He also bought a first edition of *Paradise Lost*, lot 88, 5*s*., Seven Pieces on Shorthand, lot 135, 3*s*., and Lewis's[*] manuscripts on printing, and his *Life of Caxton* etc., lot 374, 9*s*.6*d*.

His bibliographical books

On the 10th day of the West sale, there were 22 lots of 'Typographical History, Antiquities and Fragments of various sizes'. Herbert bought lot 1917, 'Portraits & Devices of Old English Printers – a wall of antiquarian English paper marks', £2.2*s*. Bibliography in our sense had not yet been invented and reference tools were thin on the ground; just how thin is seen by comparing Herbert's collection with that of the printer and Caxton historian, William Blades (1824-1890), who began his book-buying some 50 years after Herbert's death: 'He began when he was a printer's apprentice to buy up all the books he could – that is, all he came across, and all his slender purse would permit – on the art to which his life was to be devoted.'[34] The black-letter mania of the early 19th century had put Caxton collecting out of reach of men of middling means, but the development of photo-lithography offered respectable working substitutes, and Blades's library contained nearly as many Caxton facsimiles as Herbert's did originals. 'Mr Blades does not purchase Caxtons,' he announced in *How to Tell a Caxton*, 1870. In the age of expanding railway travel, it was possible for an enthusiastic young man to find time, even in an extremely busy life, to travel up and down the country, or even to hop over to the continent, to examine Caxtons and original documents in private and public collections and he had the added advantage of an increasing range of reference works available to him; Herbert, by comparison, was hampered by the primitive transport of his day, and was, besides, doing most of his research at the end of his life when he was over-old to cope with too many arduous, bone-shaking coach journeys – even if the use of other gentlemen's libraries and the loan of books could have supplied all his needs. He had to have his own copies of the books he required for his research, and he was a bibliophile whereas Blades was a practising printer, much of whose trade was in security work, and his real interest was in analysing types and investigating the techniques used by the early printers. Herbert, on the other hand, we may conjecture was not much interested in this aspect of printing history – he did not attempt to expand Ames's seminal type identification as a method of dating undated Caxtons, and his excuse for ending at 1600, 'the term which Mr Ames assigned to himself' seems rather lame: 'The history of the mechanical part has been fully handled by Mr Mores in his History of Letter-Founders' (Preface xii). He seems not to have had Moxon's *Mechanick Exercises* (1683-4), but he did have Watson's *History of the Art of Printing* (1713) (lot 752 in the Arrowsmith and Bowley sale). He seems to have bought such bibliographical tools as were available, if we assume (and I think we can) that the bibliographical works in the dispersal sales were his personal books – of course, the numerous annotated works were so. He had the standard histories of printing – the *raison d'être* of his entire collection was Ames's *Typographical Antiquities*, 1749 – but he also had Meerman, *An Account of the Origin of Printing*, 1775, Mattaire, *Annales Typographiques*, 1789, Palmer's *General History of Printing*, 1733, Lewis's *Original of the Life of Caxton* (he had Lewis's own copy annotated in manuscript, bought at Tutet's sale, and annotated further) and Bowyer & Nichols, *Origin of Printing*, 1774, 'with Manuscript Observations by Mr Herbert', as Arrowsmith and Bowley noted, lot 476. Thomas Warton's *History of Literature* 'supplied' Herbert 'with much information' and he thought that 'there needed no apology' for quoting Warton's 'observations at length, so closely connected with our subject,' (Preface to the *Antiquities* vi). He annotated the 1st edition, 3 vol., 1774-81, which appeared in the Arrowsmith and Bowley sale, lot 810, 'with MS. Notes by Mr Herbert' and also the first volumes of the second edition of which only three out of four volumes, 1775-1806, were published in his lifetime.[35] He had a good collection of library catalogues – Castley's Catalogue of the MSS of the King's Library, 1734 (lot 172 in the Arrowsmith and Bowley sale), Catalogue of Pamphlets in the Harleian Library n.d. (lot 174), and the *Catalogus Bibliotheca Bodleiana*, in 2 vols., both the 1674 and 1738 editions.

His transcribing of imperfect copies and annotating of others

In the absence of adequate bibliographical tools, Herbert manufactured his own by interleaving existing works and annotating them extensively. He was, even by the standards of days which knew not the photocopier or the word processor, a formidable copyist. One of his greatest feats was to transcribe the entire Stationers' Company Register A and Liber B which he was allowed to borrow for a few months in 1780, and again in 1790.[36] In 1781 Richard Farmer gave him 'free use of a copy of Maunsell's Catalogue, with large MS additions by the late Archbishop Harsnet and Mr Thomas Baker[(*)]...and by the latter bequeathed to the Public Library at Cambridge'. Herbert painstakingly copied out all Harsnet's and Baker's notes, running to some 160 pages, adding 'WH' against those books which he possessed but leaving 'penes me' for those so marked by Baker. 'That must have taken him quite some time', was Professor Corsten's comment.[37] It was invaluable to a bibliophile who had to make do without *BLC*, Hain, *STC* and all the rest of the tools we take for granted today. Perhaps, after those two, Herbert's transcription of 'Books in the custody of Mr Thomas Martin...which are not in Mr Ames's History of Printing...communicated to me by Mr Fenn Esq...at East Dereham, in Norfolk 16 Sept 1778',[38] seems a small matter. Not so his interleaved Ames, and his own revision interleaved and bound in six volumes, which contains many thousands of annotations, which he was still working on when he died. Another mammoth task was his so-called manuscript of the *Antiquities*, which is, in reality, an extensive common-place book, a six-volume store-house with collations of books to be included in the *Antiquities*, lists of books sent for sale through Isaac Herbert, correspondence with printers and others, and drafts of part of the *Antiquities* and much else.[39] Other working papers included a 'collection of small paper books, in which he took some extracts of such books as were discovered since his publication, when in London, or elsewhere, and marked on the outside with the Hebrew Alphabet'. (Dibdin p.86.)[40]

Condition, conservation and binding

Even in the 18th century, Caxtons did not grow on trees, and Herbert bought many imperfect copies of black-letter and other early books, some of which had been 'made perfect by manuscript'; others he completed himself in the same way. It is generally agreed that his library was 'Perhaps seldom equalled in the riches of black-letter literature', but the look of his books does not seem to have concerned him over-much and he probably left his early books as they were when acquired – we have no means of knowing what he did about new books. We have no extant bills for binding, or correspondence concerning purchases, and have to draw our conclusions from books of known Herbert provenance or occasional mention of bindings in the dispersal sales, more often 'boards' or 'boards uncut' than 'russia' or 'elegant in russia, gilt leaves'. He did not bother to have his books presenting a uniform appearance on the shelves in the custom of his day – but not ours – and the only suggestion of a prestige binding is the rare indulgence of the Herbert wyvern crest tooled on the top cover of a book. Nor is he likely to have taken measures to conserve his bindings, and the *Profitable Book to take out Spots and Staines in Silkes, Velvets, Linnen and Woollen, to dresse Leather, etc etc*, 1596 (lot 598 in the Arrowsmith and Bowley sale) was not acquired for practical use.

The arrangement of his library

We do not know what sort of catalogue, if any, Herbert had and the only evidence we have of how he kept track of his books or how they stood on the shelves is in the consignments of books which he sent to his nephew for sale, between June 1793 and January 1795. We know nothing of his domestic arrangements on Old London Bridge or at Goulston Square; but at Cheshunt, according to Dibdin,'he built one of the wings of his house expressly for the reception of his books; and here he used to sit, under a circular skylight...'. Dibdin speaks of his 'passion for books *and antiquities*' (the *italics* are mine) and although he did not bid for any of the medals in West's Museum of Curiosities nor at several other large sales of medals, he specified medals in his will. Were they laid out in a case in his library? Were the objects he bought at the West sale destined for library furniture? – 'a small but curious amber cabinet', lot 8, 3 guineas – a 'stone with Hebrew characters', lot 17, £2.7s. – 'a curious ivory ball', unnumbered lot, £1.8s. – 'a large salver enamelled, on copper, with Apollo and Daphne', lot 32, 16s.6d., and 'a large pan and cover on feet', lot 63, £5.6d. (We note, by the way, that each cost him more than 'MS Directions on how to make coloured and gilded letters, such as are to be met with in old Ms. by

Elizabeth Elstob', lot 66, 5s.6d.) Did he adorn his book-cases with classical busts?

The mystery of the dispersal

In his will of 5 May 1792 Herbert left his house, with lands, household effects, and 'books, MSS, maps, charts, prints, medals, coins, curiosities' to his wife, Phillippa, and, if she died without issue, to Isaac Herbert. It has always been taken that the books were disposed of in three posthumous sales, 1796-1798,[41] but this cannot be the whole story. These three sales contain about 5,000 works offered in single lots, including many unidentified properties, booksellers' stock and unsold items slipped in among Herbert's books; many of known Herbert provenance are conspicuous by their absence and may have been retained by the widow.

Some mystery surrounds Isaac Herbert and his part in the dispersal. As we have already mentioned, at the end of his life, William Herbert sent his nephew consignments of books for sale; Volume I, pages 1-19, of the manuscript of the *Typographical Antiquities* consists of lists of books variously headed: 'To I* H 6 June 1793...28 & 29 Aug. 1793...I* H by Mr. Whacket' (the carrier?) '...French books sent to I* H'; by this is pencilled 'not yet sent' and, on page 11, 'sent to Norton's 1 Jan 1795 to sell on account of WH or return'. Many of the books are price-coded (for example, 't/n t/a n/p') as well as having ticks, mostly in pencil, beside them. It is significant that, during the same period, Isaac Herbert was issuing catalogues of 'select and considerable collections of books, very lately purchased...the price of every book is printed in the catalogue...(to be annually continued)...'. The first was 'for the year...1793'. Two more followed in 1794 and early 1795 but the series petered out after Herbert's death with the catalogue of 10 March 1796, which contained 2,488 items. We might be able to crack Herbert's price code if the books in the manuscript lists were compared with the titles and prices in the catalogues and the annotation of item 784 in that for 1795 – *Ponet on Politick Power...10s.6d.* – which is catalogued with the note – 'Note in this tract by Mr Herbert, "it cost me 15s. and yet I had it by the interest of a friend"' might tell us more. A close comparison could reveal a good deal about the bookselling activities of uncle and nephew; was Herbert still trading as a bookseller, using his nephew as his agent, was he beginning to dismantle his library in his lifetime, or was he helping the young man get established as a dealer? Did Isaac Herbert's catalogues cease in 1796, because, with his uncle's death, the fount dried up and the guiding hand was withdrawn? Where did he get the rest of the Herbert books which went to the sale-rooms two years later? Did Isaac

Herbert write to Dibdin from abroad because he had fled from creditors? The answer may partly be found in the codicil to William Herbert's will, dated 19 December 1794, revoking a former injunction – Isaac Herbert, who had already been advanced £500, was 'to be advanced no further money for carrying on his trade as a bookseller'. The uncle knew how to order his life, but evidently the nephew was a failure, if not positively a bad lot.

Conclusion: the man and his books

We have a good many facts about Herbert: we have his books, annotations and notebooks in his distinctive hand in abundance; a very few letters written by him, and a good many written to him.[42] The only first-hand account is Richard Gough's obituary in the *Gentleman's Magazine*, supplemented by Dibdin's graphic but unreliable description of his appearance and character, derived from Isaac Herbert or some other gossip. Analysis of his book purchases gives us the pattern of his bookbuying as he progressed from hydrography, books on travel and topography in a variety of languages through to the history of English books, and, in a rough and ready way, provides us with a kind of bibliographical 'identikit'. The picture emerges of a self-effacing man who gave instruction in his will that his body 'be committed to the earth whence it came with as little pomp and ceremony as may be'. At the same time there emerges a highly motivated, shrewd and organised man; and this in spite of some seeming disorganisation as he wrestled with his grand design of extending Ames, a project which could not be kept to the deadline he had set – but only an organised man would have met that deadline at all – a cautious man who kept his bibliographical passion more or less under control. By the end of his life he was wealthy enough to buy fine books in quantity, but even the richest can overspend, and he never forgot sound business principles – he might pay for what he bought from private wealth or money earned from dealing and publishing, but he seems to have eked out extra profit by buying for others at auction and by fining down his library by selling books which no longer served his needs, which, at the end of his life, were directed to more and more research and enlargement of the *Typographical Antiquities*.

References

1. [William Beloe] *The sexagenarian*, 2 vols, 1817, i, 197.
2. The sources for Herbert's life are:
   (1) Richard Gough's obituary, *Gentleman's Magazine*. July 1795, reprinted with small variations, LA v 264-6.

(2) T.F. Dibdin, 'Some account of William Herbert' prefaced to his edition of the *Typographical Antiquities*, 1809-10, which lifts whole passages from Gough, but adds considerable detail whose source is either Dibdin's imagination or correspondence with Isaac Herbert, who seems to have fled abroad after his uncle's death.

(3) *DNB* which draws heavily on Gough and Dibdin.

(4) Manuscript sources itemised below pp.156.

3. I consider that one dated book-plate (see p.142) pinpoints 1745 as the latest date of Herbert's return to London.

4. I am indebted to Andrew Cook for this information.

5. Bridge House Rentals vols. 43 & 44 (1741-65), where Herbert is described as a print-seller.

6. John Pace, bound 3 August 1751, later set up as print-seller in Broadway, Westminster; Thomas Wright, bound 20 July 1756, became a print-seller in Great Eastcheap.

7. *A chronological and historical account from the first building a bridge across the River Thames, from London to Southwark, 'till the late conflagration of the temporary bridge*, the 11th of April, 1758. Sold by William Herbert, on the remains of London Bridge [1758]. My source is ESTC; I have not seen a copy.

8. William Herbert, *A new directory for the East-Indies, with general and particular charts for the navigation of those seas: wherein the French Neptune oriental has been chiefly consider'd and examined*...the second edition, London, printed for the editor, 1759.

William Nichelson, *Sundry remarks and observations made in a voyage to the* East-Indies, *on board...the Elizabeth...1758, to...1764. With the necessary directions for sailing to and from India ...Being a proper supplement to the New Directory for the East-Indies*. By William Nichelson...London, printed for W. Herbert, by T. Spilsbury, 1764. The 4th and 5th editions, 1775 and 1780, were published by Henry Gregory.

9. Herbert's interleaved and annotated copy of the 1765 edition was auctioned by Arrowsmith and Bowley, Nov. 1798, lot 585.

10. *The ancient and present state of Glocestershire*. By Sir Robert Atkyns [the younger]...The second edition...London, printed in the year MDXII, Reprinted by T. Spilsbury for W. Herbert; sold by J. Millan; T. Payne; Davis and Reyners [& 12 others in London and 1 in Gloucester] 1768.

Isaac Herbert offered copies on his 1795 catalogue at 5 guineas, and unsold copies were offered by Arrowsmith and Bowley, 1798.

The history of Herbert's purchase and republication of Atkyns, is told, LA v 258, and repeated by Dibdin and *DNB*.

11. He was freed at Drapers' Hall by patrimony, 16 Nov 1748, and paid quarterage as a dyer; admitted to the livery, 1763; Court Assistant, 1783 and attended his first court, 30 Sept. having been made 4th Warden, 26 Sept; 2nd Warden, 27 Sept 1791; Master Warden, 7 Oct 1792.

12. Dibdin says he retired, 1769; the Drapers' record a change of address from Goulston Square to Cheshunt, 1773, and letters begin to be thus headed that year, though he seems to have kept a London base until 1776.

13. The White-Herbert correspondence is Bodley Eng.Lett. 359.

14. IL iv 545-550.

15. LA v 258.

16. Sir Peter Thompson's copy of the catalogue, B.L. 11904.g.24.

17. According to his statements in the *Antiquities*, Ames owned 19 Caxtons and 5 fragments; there were a total of 5 in the dispersal sale.

18. Herbert shared with Luke Hansard the idiosyncrasy of writing the first person with lower case 'i'.
19. Mr Sokol confirms that the book-plate was the anonymous one of which I sent him a photocopy.
20. IL iv 540.
21. B.L. Add.MSS 5834 f.100, reprinted LA i 701.
22. Letters from Herbert are rare; this one, written from Cheshunt, 1 Jan. 1788, is National Library of Scotland, MS 1709, and was transcribed for me by Arnold Hunt on a visit there.
23. Brian North Lee investigated the book-plate for me; he found that there was an example dated 1745 and signed by the engraver, John June, in the Franks Collection, British Library; he also found it referred to by various writers on book-plates and described in Warren's *Guide to the Study of Book-Plates*, 1880 as 'A very exceptional book-plate signed J. June, 1745...the frame-work of the shield is the foreign analogue of chippendale, which may be called Rococo. The landscape accessories, a birch tree on the right, a cypress on the left, with a brook flowing out from underneath, the escutcheon frame, are at this period on the English book-plate most unusual. A single cupid is seated as a quasi-supporter on the right of the shield. The plate is anonymous, but belongs to the Herbert family' (Warren, late Lord de Tabley, 173). Brian agreed that it was a very early example of the Chippendale style of book-plate and further quoted from a letter in his possession from V.M. Turnbull, Cambridge, 31 August 1956 to Tom Owen: 'I have had a copy of [Herbert's anonymous plate] for over 40 years, and...recently...discovered a copy of it in...Dibdin's *Typographical Antiquities*, not quite an exact copy & without the artist's signature'. John June is not recorded as engraving any other book-plate.
24. Herbert's book-plate is in the following volumes:
      (1) Stationers' Hall: Herbert's three notebooks transcribing the Stationers' Company's early registers has his book-plate in each book, one overlaid by that of George Chalmers who bought the notebooks at the Arrowsmith and Bowley dispersal sale.
      (2) B.L. G.19928 (in Thomas Grenville's binding, his book-label in front board, with annotations by him and others) John Field and Thomas Wilcox, *An admonition to the parliament*, 1572 (STC 10847, Herbert, *Antiquities* III 1631) bound in with *A second admonition to the parliament* (STC 10849, Herbert, *Antiquities* III 1631) and *Certain articles, collected and taken...by the byshops out of a litle boke entitled an Admonition...*(STC 10850, Herbert, *Antiquities* III 1632). In addition to Herbert's book-plate there is his signature 'W. Herbert 1772' and note; 'it was twice printed; i have both editions'.
      (3) B.L. IC.4508: Ludolphi *Vita Christi Coloniae* [1481] with 'W. Herbert 1779' and book-plate on second flyleaf.
      (4) B.L. C.11.c.10: Chaucer, *Troilus and Criseyde*, Caxton, 1483 (STC 5094, De Ricci n.30 & p.164, one of two copies owned by Herbert and sold by Isaac Herbert, 1795, no.413).
      (5) and (6)Two other Grenville-Herbert books are said to have the Herbert book-plate; at time of writing they were at the binder.
      (7) *The Thre Kynges of Coleyne*, 1526, now in North America.
      His wyvern crest is on the top cover of:
      (1) B.L. G 5932: R. Harvey, *Philadelphus*, London 1593.
      (2) No.29. Boethius, *de consolationae philosophiae...*Cawood, 1556. A page torn from an unidentified bookseller's catalogue, 'among a large box [of E.G. Duff

papers] loose notes on armorial bindings' found in the University Library, Cambridge by Arnold Hunt.

    (3)   ULC Syn.8.57.88: T.R. *A philospicall discourse entituled, The anchorite of the minde*, 1576, contains 'W. Herbert 1771' on the title page, and Herbert's crest.

25. Frans Corsten, *A Catalogue of the Library of Thomas Baker*, 1990.
26. ULC Munby c.84. I am grateful to Arnold Hunt for tracking this marked and priced catalogue down for me.
27. I am indebted to Nest Davies for this suggestion.
28. LA v 391. Andrew Ducarel extended Ames's list to 1776, and it was added to further by Mark Cephas Tutet and others.
29. MS Douce, *Douce Legacy*, 1990, p.108.
30. Bodley, Nichols collection b.12, f 159/6029.
31. Marked copy of *Bibliotheca Westiana*, Feb. 1773 ULC 7880.c.105.
32. Marked copy of *Bibliotheca Ratcliffiana*, 1776, ULC 7880.c.98 2.
33. Marked copy of Tutet's sale catalogue, B.L. 821.g.12 (1).
34. St Bride Foundation Institute, John Southwood, *Catalogue of the William Blades Library*, 1899, p.iv.
35. H.G.Bohn offered the second edition for sale 'with a few MS notes by W. Herbert...' on his Catalogue of Books, vol.I 1848, Bibliography section 437. This was a reissue of his 1841 Guinea Catalogue. I am grateful to Esther Potter to pointing it out to me, and lending me her copy.
36. 'Stationers' Company bibliographers...Ames to Arber' in *Pioneers in Bibliography* in this series, 1988, pp.44-6.
37. Arrowsmith and Bowley, lot 628, noted that it was 'interleaved with considerable MS additions from Archbishop Harsnett, and T. Baker's copy, by Mr Herbert...'. Herbert's copy is now at the Huntington Library, San Marino, California.
38. ULC Add 3393.
39. ULC Add 3313-8, purchased at Sotheby sale of Phillipps MSS, 1895.
40. B.L. Add.MS 18202.
41. *The List of English Book Sales...1676*, and Coral and Munby's *British Book Sales to 1800* both give these three sales only.
42. David Stoker tantalised me by telling me that five Herbert letters and a receipt were among lot 120 of Sotheby's *Catalogue of the valuable library of John Tudor Frere*, Feb 14-18, 1896.

Acknowledgements

This paper, which is very much work in progress, makes use of only a proportion of the material assembled with the help of many. I am particularly indebted to Arnold Hunt and Alison Shell, who, out of kindness, were really unofficial research assistants. I also thank the following for help and advice: Vivienne Aldous, of the Corporation of London Record Office, Geoffrey Groom of the Bodleian Library, Andrew Cook of the India Office Library, Nest Davies, Christine Ferdinand, David Hall, Lotte Hellinga, Philippa Marks of the British Library, Paul Morgan, Brian North-Lee, David Pearson of the British Library, Esther Potter, and Tom Wareham, Education Officer at the Drapers' Company.

Biographical Index

Key

+ appears under the initials given in Herbert's list of owners of books in annotated Ames (see p.158).
§ mentioned in preface to Herbert's edition of the *Typographical Antiquities*, 3 vols, 1785-90.
# Original subscriber to Herbert's *Antiquities*.

+ *Joseph Ames* FSA (1689-1759), (+JA) ship chandler, antiquary, first secretary of the Society of Antiquaries, author of the *Typographical Antiquities*, 1749.

Thomas Baker (1656-1740), antiquary, non-juror, Fellow of St John's College, Cambridge, to whom he left his library.

+ *Sir Joseph Banks* FRS (1742-1820), President of the Royal Society, explorer, naturalist, bibliophile, whose books are preserved in the British Library.

+ *William Cole* MA, FSA (1714-1782), antiquary, lived at Waterbeach, Cambs (1767-79) and Milton, Cambs (1770-1782), 'furnished his friends with materials for historical and antiquarian books'; left his Cambridge and local history collections to the British Museum.

#+ *Alexander Dalrymple* FRS (1727-1808), (+) Hydrographer to the East India Company, (1779-95) and to the Admiralty (1795-1808), bibliophile whose vast library was auctioned by King and Lochee 29 May and 6 November (29 days) 1809.

#+ *Lockyer Davis* (1719-1791), bookseller, Master of the Stationers' Company (1779) translated la Rochefoucault.

#+ *Andrew Coltee Ducarel* FRS, FSA,DCL, (1713-1785), lawyer, antiquary, Lambeth Librarian (1757-85), arranged State Papers (1763), bibliophile.

#+ *Richard Farmer* FSA, DD, etc (1735-1797), (+RF) Master of Emmanuel College, Cambridge, Shakespeare scholar, bibliophile etc.

Sir John Fenn (1739-1794) (+F), Norfolk antiquary and dignitary, editor of the Paston letters, friend of Thomas Martin. Fenn's Letters, 4 vols. 1787, were for sale on Isaac Herbert's catalogue for the year 1794.

#+ *Richard Gough* FSA, FRS (1735-1809), antiquary, friend of John Nichols and contributor to the *Gentleman's Magazine*.

Isaac Herbert, (b.1772?) son of Thomas Herbert, nephew of William Herbert; bound at Stationers' Hall, 1787, to John Hayes, book- and print-seller; a premium of £105 paid by his uncle; traded from Pall Mall, 1793-4, 29 Great Russell Street, 1795-6, Holborn 1798; issued annual catalogues of books, including many of his uncle's, 1793-6; bankrupt, 10 November, 1798; fled abroad; corresponded with Dibdin after William Herbert's death.

John Hutton (d.1764), paper-stainer and 'a very sedulous collector of books', his library auctioned after his death by Paterson and Bristow, October 1764 (29 days) – 'not a single article in this collection, but what was the property of the deceased gentleman'.

Thomas King (fl.1768-1817), leading book auctioneer, in partnership with his son-in-law, Lochee (1806-17), succeeded by his son, Thomas King II.

John Lewis (1675-1747), (+L) Vicar in Thanet, antiquary and topographer of Kent, friend of Joseph Ames, encouraged Ames to write the *Typographical Antiquities*, author of the first serious life of Caxton; Herbert bought his annotated copy and his working papers at Tutet's sale.

#+ *George Mason* (1735-1806), (+GM) miscellaneous writer, lawyer, bibliophile; his library sold, 4 parts, Leigh and Sotheby, 1798 & 1799, the residue posthumously, 1807.

Thomas Newman (1692-1758), dissenting minister, son of a linen draper, pastor at Blackfriars, published theological works, his niece said to have married William Herbert.

+ *John Pinkerton* (1758-1826), Scottish antiquary, historian and forger of Scottish ballads, friend of Horace Walpole and Gibbon.

+ *John Ratcliffe* (d.1776), (+RF) chandler in Bermondsey, book collector, friend of Herbert and William White, his library sold posthumously by Christie, 1776 (9 days).

Sir Peter Thompson FRS, FSA (1698-1770), (+Sir PT) merchant, collector, friend of Ames, Oldys and William Bowyer.

#+ *Mark Cephas Tutet* FSA (1733-1785), (+T) merchant, antiquary, bibliophile and friend and executor of Dr Ducarel; his 'small but valuable library' sold 1786.

+ *James West* FRS, FSA (1704?-1772), (+JW) politician, lawyer, antiquary, collector, President of the Royal Society, his vast library and museum of curiosities sold in 3 sales, 1773.

#+ *William White* (c.1733-1815), (+WW) possibly printseller and publisher of Angel Court, Westminster, friend and business associate of Herbert, Ratcliffe, Mason and others; moved to Crickhowell, near Abergavenny, *c*.1770, sold a small quantity of undistinguished books through Thomas King, 1808.

Sources

PRIMARY SOURCES

Ames's interleaved copy of the *Typographical Antiquities*, annotated by him and further annotated by Herbert, B.L. C.60.0.5 (cited as annotated Ames).

Herbert's interleaved and annotated copy of his edition of the *Typographical Antiquities*, further annotated by Dibdin, B.L. C.133.ee.2 (cited as annotated Herbert).

Manuscript of [Herbert's revision of] the *Typographical Antiquities*, 6 vols, ULC 3313-8 (cited as Antiquities manuscript).

Andrew Maunsell, *Catalogue of English Printed Bookes...of Divinity and Science...* 2 parts, 1595, annotated by Archbishop Harsnett and Thomas Baker, and copied by William Herbert. The Harsnett/Baker copy; Herbert's transcript Huntington Library, (cited as Herbert's Maunsell).

Books in the Custody of Thomas Martin which are not mentioned in Ames's *Typographical Antiquities* 1778. ULC Add 3393 (cited as Herbert/Martin).

William Herbert's notebooks on printing, lettered with the Hebrew alphabet. B.L. Add.MS 1802 A-W.

Letters, mainly to William Herbert in: the Nichols collection, Bodleian Library and B.L. Manuscript Room (much reprinted with variations by John Nichols in IL).

SELECT MARKED AND PRICED SALE CATALOGUES

Library of Joseph Ames, Langford, 5 May 1760. Sir Peter Thompson's marked copy B.L. 11904.g.24.

Catalogue of the large and curious library of Mr John Hutton, late of St Paul's Churchyard, Paterson and Bristow, 22 October 1764, 28 evenings,marked copy ULC Munby c.84.

Bibliotheca Ratcliffiana... Christie, 27 March 1776. 24 days, perhaps William Herbert's marked copy ULC 7880.c.98 (2).

Catalogue of the library of Thomas Martin of Palgrave, extracts printed in *Memoirs of the Life of Thomas Gent*, pp.263-5.

Catalogue of the large and justly admired museum of curiosities of James West... Christie, Feb 17 1773 (7 days) B.L.821.e.25 & 270 k.7.

Biliotheca Westiana... Paterson and Langford, Feb 3, 1773 (24 days) ULC 7880.c.105.

Library of Mark Cephas Tutet, J. Gerard 15 Feb. 1786 B.L. 821.g.12.

A catalogue of several select and considerable collections of books, very lately purchased; comprising a general assortment of antient and modern literature...the price of every book is printed in the catalogue. They will continue on sale till the end of the year, by I. Herbert, bookseller...catalogues (to be annually continued) may be had at the place of sale... 1793 Bodley 2593.f.1(1).

Isaac Herbert's catalogue of books for the year 1794. no.6 Pall-Mall Bodley 1593.f.1(2).

Catalogue of books in various languages...included part of the...library of the late Mr William Herbert...which are on sale...by Isaac Herbert, bookseller no.29 Great Russell Street (removed from Pall-Mall) 1795. Bodley Mus.Bibl.III 8o 287 (1).

Catalogue of the library of William Herbert, Leigh and Sotheby, March 10 1796, Sotheby film part 1 reel 10 (W.A. Jackson's copy).

Catalogue of the entire and curious library of a late well-known collector [MS: 'Mr Herbert'] *removed from his country residence...which will be sold by auction by Mr Postan 2 April 1798 and 7 following days...* Bodley Mus. Bibl.III 8o 287 (2).

Catalogue of a choice and valuable library, the property of a gentleman [MS: chiefly Herbert's Remains and the property of Arrowsmith] *to which is added the...manuscripts of...the late Mr William Herbert...Arrowsmith and Bowley, Nov.21, 1798* (5 days) Bodley Douce CC 394(4) & Mus. Bibl.III 8o 287(3).

[London] Bridge House Rentals and Accounts, vols. 43 (1741-1755) and 44 (1755-1765) Corporation of London Record Office, Comp B.H. Deed: Box 14, no.5.

MS index to bindings, court minutes, freedoms, 1748-1822, printed livery lists, 1782 and 1787, Drapers' Hall.

The will of William Herbert PRO Probate 11, 1259.

SELECT SECONDARY AND PRINTED SOURCES

Joseph Ames, *Typographical antiquities: being an historical account of printing in England*, 1749 (cited as Ames' *Antiquities*).

Joseph Ames, *Typographical antiquities; or an historical account of the origin and progress of printing in Great Britain and Ireland, augmented by William Herbert of Cheshunt, Herts.* 3 vols, 1785-90 (cited as Herbert, *Antiquities* or *The Antiquities*).

Joseph Ames, *The Typographical antiquities of Great Britain*, revised by T.F. Dibdin, 4 vols, 1811-19 (Preface cited as Dibdin or Dibdin's Preface).

E.G. Duff, *Pedigrees of early English books, notes on Herbert's books*, MS ULC Add 8602.

John Nichols, *Literary anecdotes of the eighteenth century*, 9 vols, 1812-15 (cited as LA).

John Nichols, *Illustrations of the literary history of the eighteenth century*, 8 vols, 1817-58 (cited IL).

[A.W. Pollard] *List of Catalogues of English Book Sales 1676-1900 now in the British Museum*, 1915.

A.N.L. Munby and Leonore Coral, *British Book Sale Catalogues 1676-1800, a Union List*, 1977.

Seymour de Ricci, *English Collectors of Books & Manuscripts (1530-1930) and their marks of ownership*, 1930.

Seymour de Ricci, *A Census of Caxtons*, 1909.

Initials of owners of books listed in annotated Ames

Joseph Ames's annotated copy of the *Typographical Antiquities*, 1749, which William Herbert bought from Sir Peter Thompson, 1760 and annotated further; it passed to Dibdin, then went to the Museum from J.T. Stanesby: (B.L. C.60.05). On the verso of the marbled front wrapper is the following list of initials of owners whose books are cited in *Ames-revised-Herbert*.

* indicates that Herbert bought at the sale.

RF	Mr John Ratcliffe *	BC	Bibliotheca Croftsiana
JW	James West *	GM	George Mason
TR	Thomas Rawlinson	SH	Samuel Hayes (bookseller of Oxford Street)
WB	William Bayntun		
WH	William Herbert	RM	Rowe Mores
WW	William White	AM	Andrew Maunsell
DG	David Garrick	WEP	Warton's History of English Poetry
RF	Richard Farmer – library sold 1798	PAP	Percy's Ancient Poetry
		L	Lewis's Life of Caxton
TP	Thomas Payne's catalogue	D	Alexander Dalrymple
BAC	Bibliotheca Anglia Curiosa	GS	George Steevens
ML	Michael Lort	TP	Thomas Pearson
G	Harleian Miscellany	V	Mr Voet
OSW	Oldys' Life of Sir W. Raleigh	SS	New Ann Office
WC	William Collins, (bookseller d.1801)	Pref to J & S	Johnson's Shakespeare
		R	Mr Reed
H	Sir John Hawkins – library catalogue not in BLC	2BC	little memo books with my MS remarks
R	Robert New	BTB	Bibliotheca Beauclerk (Topham Beauclerk)
BMF	Bibliotheca Monastica Fleetwoodiana		
M	Mr Mole		*On interleaf:* 'list of marks used by gentlemen when they had look'd over writings, or books':
MP	Morgan's Phoenix (John Morgan. Phoenix Britannicus 1732)		
H	Catalogue of pamphlets in Harleian library	CM	Mr Martin of Palgrave, Norfolk (Suffolk?)
LL	Lambeth Palace	+	Francis Blomefield when extracted: B FB when copied
AL	Ames's list of Bibles		
Sir PT	Sir Peter Thompson	=	Mr Parkin (Charles? 1689-1765)
BA	Bibliotheca Askeriana *	#	Mr Jos. Baldwin
T	Mr Tutet, (Mark Cephas Tutet) *	B+B	Mr Beaupré Bell (1704-45)
F	John Fenn	AN	Mr Anthony Norris (1711-86)
TM	Thomas Martin	#	Bp
JA	Joseph Ames's papers		
JB	John Baynes		
CBH	Catalogo Bibliotheca Harlieana		

Index

Orford, R. & T. (bookplates), 64
Osborne, Thomas (bookseller), 7
Overbury, *Sir* Thomas, 116
Oxford (book sale at), 6
Oxinden collection (plays), 114, 129*n*.

Paas, C. and A. (engravers), 56, 57, 75*n*.
Page, *Sir* Henry, 64, 75*n*.
Paget, William, 4th *Lord* (library), 118-119
Parker, *Archbishop*, 36
Parker, Samuel, 128
Parkin, Charles, 102
Paston Letters, 99, 100, 105
Paterson, Samuel (book auctioneer), 7-8
Pawlowski, Gustave, 82
Payne, Roger (bookbinder), 36, 37
Payne, Thomas (bookseller), 27, 104, 157
Peckard, Peter, 71, 76*n*.
Pembroke, *Earl* of, 29, 35
Penrose, Boise (collection), 88
Pepys, Samuel, 25, 27, 28, 32, 39*n*., 43, 126, 128
Pepysian Library, Cambridge, 113, 139
Peterborough Literary Club, 66, 76*n*.
Petrarch, Francesco, 127
Phillips, *Sir* Richard (publisher), 27
Phillips, *Sir* Thomas, 82
Pickering, William (publisher), 26, 32
Pinkerton, John, 140, 155
Pius II, *Pope*, 84
Plays, in gentlemen's libraries, 114-115, 119, 120, 124
Plume, Thomas (book collector), viii, 1-3, 13
Plume Library, Maldon, 3
Pollard, Graham, 32
Polwarth, John (bookbinder), 36
Potter, Esther, viii, x, 25-41, 153*n*.
Price, John (Bodley's librarian), 140
Prideaux, Sarah, 36
Prynne, John, 2
Prynne, William, 121
Public Record Office, London, 95, 96, 123
Pynson, Richard (books printed by), 142, 145

Quaritch, Bernard (bookseller), 80-89

Rabelais, François, 118

Ramsden, Charles, 34, 40*n*.
Ratcliffe, John, 138, 144, 145, 155, 158
Rawlinson, Richard (book collector), 6, 7, 9, 101, 125
Rawlinson, Thomas (book collector), 6, 158
Rees, Eiluned, 36, 40*n*.
Rivington, James (publisher), 33
Robiquet, John (bookbinder), 35
Roscoe, William (librarian & collector), 29
Rothschild, Edmond de, 84
Roxburghe Club, 86
Roxburghe Sale (1812), 28
Royal Geographical Society, London, 79
Royal Society, 126
Ruling, in books (17th century), 28
Ruskin, John (collection), 84

St Paul's Churchyard, 6, 10, 25, 32, 71, 156
St Paul's Coffee House, 6
Samuel, David (bookseller), 99
Sandars Lectures, Cambridge, 85
Scott, *Sir* Walter, 19, 23, 24*n*.
Scrope, Joshua (book-plates), 56
Seaman, *Dr* Lazarus (collector), 4, 6
Sheldon, Ralph (collector), 114
Shelf-marks, 65, 76*n*.
Sidney, *Sir* Philip, 99, 114
Simpson, Thomas (joiner), 32
Skinner, *Rev.* John (antiquary), 17, 66, 68
Skipwith, *Sir* Francis (book-plate), 63
Smith, George, 78
Smollett, Tobias, 33-34
Society of Antiquaries, London, 106, 107*n*.
Somerset, *Duke* of (book-plates), 63
Sotheby's (auctioneers), 8, 11, 14*n*., 77-89, 138, 157
Sotheby, Samuel Leigh, 14*n*.
Sotheran (booksellers), 80
Spalding, Gentlemen's Society, 66, 76*n*., 108*n*.
Spencer, *Earl*, 18
See also Althorp
Spilsbury, T. (printer), 134, 151*n*.
Spitzer sale, 81
Spufford, *Dr* Margaret, 113
Stafford, Humphrey, *1st Duke* of Buckingham, 81
Stanley, *Sir* John (library of), 8